CONCILIUM

Religion in the Eighties

CONCILIUM

Editorial Directors

Concilium 157 (7/1982): Church Order

MAY CHURCH MINISTERS BE POLITICIANS?

Edited by
Peter Huizing
and
Knut Walf

English Language Editor
Marcus Lefébure

T. & T. CLARK LTD.
Edinburgh

THE SEABURY PRESS
New York

September 1982
T. & T. Clark Ltd., 36 George Street, Edinburgh EH2 2LQ
ISBN: 0 567 30037 4

The Seabury Press, 815 Second Avenue, New York, NY 10017
ISBN: 0 8164 2388 1

Library of Congress Catalog Card No.: 81 85844

Printed in Scotland by William Blackwood & Sons Ltd., Edinburgh

Concilium: Monthly except July and August
Subscriptions 1982: UK and Rest of the World £27·00, postage and handling included; USA and Canada, all applications for subscriptions and enquiries about *Concilium* should be addressed to The Seabury Press, 815 Second Avenue, New York, NY 10017, USA.

CONTENTS

Editorial

THE 'CHURCH in the modern world' is not the same Church that Gratian, the monk and canon lawyer, described in 1140 or thereabouts, when he wrote: 'There are two kinds of Christians—spiritual Christians (in the Church) and lay Christians (in the world).' The problem of 'priests (= the "official Church") and politics' is only one aspect of the mystery of the 'Church in the modern world'.

ON THE PART OF THE PRIESTS

According to the *Codex Iuris Canonici* of 1917-1918, members of the clergy are obliged to have permission from Rome before they can accept functions in the government or in civil administration or, in countries in which that is forbidden by Rome, before they can stand for election as representatives of the people. Elsewhere priests must have permission from their own ordinary or from the ordinary of the place where the election is to take place. These statutes also apply to religious (see Canons 139, §§ 2 and 4; 592).

In connection with the secular and political activities of priests, the 1971 Synod of Bishops stated, in their second general assembly, that priests are not of this world, but are witnesses to and ministers of the other life. In concrete situations, however, such activities are permissible, in so far as they are able to serve the mission of the Church, for people to whom the gospel has not yet been preached and for the Christian community, in accordance with the judgement of the bishop after consulting his priests and, if necessary, the conference of bishops. Together with the whole Church, priests also have to plan their work for the defence of human rights, full personal development, justice and peace and at the same time they ought to help lay people to form their consciences. Like all citizens, they also have a right to make political choices, but not as the only legitimate ones and even less by means of political occupations or alliances. They are not permitted to take part in active party political struggles or to function as political leaders, unless this is required in a concrete situation for the well-being of the people generally. For this they need the consent of the bishop, who may grant it after consulting with his council of priests and, if necessary, with the conference of bishops. The draft of the 1980 Code of Canon Law lays down that permission is required from Rome for bishops to undertake public functions, especially if these are in any way connected with the civil authorities, and, in countries in which Rome prohibits this, for other priests to do the same. Elsewhere, priests must have permission from their own ordinary and from the ordinary of the place where the function has to be carried out. This regulation also applies to the undertaking of such functions through election. Finally, it also applies to religious (see Canons 260, § 2, and 598).

ON THE PART OF THE LAITY

This problem was approached at the Second Vatican Council principally with the point of view of the laity in mind. It was seen as the task of the whole Church to form

Christians so that they would be able to build up temporal society in accordance with God's intentions. The 'pastors' (is this the hierarchy or priests?) have the task of proclaiming the principles concerning the goal of creation and the use of the world and of providing moral and spiritual help. The lay people for their part have the task of constructing the temporal order of society. The Church has no direct authority in this essentially lay task as citizens of this world, except in so far as principles are included within the Christian revelation concerning this task. The Church has no direct theoretical or real political authority concerning the concrete application of these principles and what can only be judged in the light of an understanding of concrete human relationships (see the *Decree on the Apostolate of the Laity,* § 7).

The *Constitution on the Church in the Modern World* also confirms the 'autonomy of earthly affairs' (§ 36). Even though the Church has no mission in the political, economic or social sphere, but only in the field of religion, it has a task, derived from its religious concern, to provide help in human society. If necessary, it has itself to take initiatives to serve man and especially the poor, by carrying out works of mercy and so on. The Church's mission as a 'sacrament', that is, the appearance and life-blood of the 'intimate union with God and of the unity of all mankind' (*Dogmatic Constitution on the Church,* § 1) is closely connected with the advancement of peace and unity in every sphere as the fruit of love (*Constitution on the Church in the Modern World,* § 42). Man, as the 'author of culture', is conscious in his autonomy of his responsibility for his fellow-men and their future (§ 55). There must be a clear distinction in the co-operation between the political community and the Church between what Catholics do in their own name as citizens and what they do in the name of the Church in union with the Church's 'shepherds' (does this mean the hierarchy or the priests of the Church?). Each is independent of the other in its own sphere and each is autonomous (§§ 75 and 76).

PRIESTLY MINISTRY AND LAY MINISTRY

On 28 February 1982, the Sunday newspapers reported that the pope had, a few days before, warned the Jesuits against tendencies to secularise the priestly ministry and to reduce it to a merely philanthropic function. The priest's ministry, the pope had stressed, was not that of a doctor, a social worker, a politician or a trade union leader. In their ministry, priests should never try to replace the function of the laity and they should above all never neglect their own specific task.

A critical columnist in the *Washington Post* noted on 6 March that he had known very many Jesuits and very few of them had been merely priests. A large number of them had been specialist teachers at his college. It had certainly not been the pope's intention to put an end to this—the very opposite was the case. In fact, however, it is very difficult to find an objective criterion by which a distinction can be made between 'priestly ministry' and 'lay ministry'. Priests have done excellent service in the missions as doctors. They have also done social work and have functioned as politicians and leaders in trade unions and other organisations. In specifically Christian groups and communities, the co-operation between priests and lay people in all spheres of religious, liturgical and social life is more complete than was believed possible a little time ago. It is to be hoped that the information that is provided in this issue of *Concilium* will act as an incentive to deeper theological reflection about this whole problem.[1]

THIS ISSUE OF *CONCILIUM*

Several fundamental aspects of the problem are considered in the first part of this issue. At the end of the eighteenth century, the Church was described as a 'perfect society' in an attempt to create a political weapon to defend the Church's judicial power. This teaching created a serious obstacle to the further development of ecclesiology until Vatican II (Granfield). A political analysis of the relationship between Church and politics (or between the priest and politics) shows how complicated this whole problem is (Lemieux). Even though demands that the Church should be 'democratised' are in principle unacceptable, it is still legitimate to ask whether the structures of the Church that are based on absolutist models really do justice to the Church as a 'community of brothers and sisters in Christ'. In this context, it is interesting to compare the use, in the style of the Roman curia, of concepts such as 'father', 'brothers', 'sons and daughters' and so on, of which only the term 'our separated brethren' is used in the evangelical sense (Gnägi). An analysis of the European 'Catholic' (or 'Christian') parties shows clearly enough that these political organs have not functioned to any great extent as the 'secular arm' in Church politics and have in fact become, as the result of a process of secularisation, 'philosophical' parties, *weltanschaunings-porteien* (Mayeur).

More factual aspects of the problem are discussed in the second part. An analysis of the class structure of the Catholic clergy in the Federal Republic of West Germany provides a model for the universally valid influence of that clergy on Church politics (Geller). Can we look forward to papal diplomacy, as represented in numerous international organisations, becoming more active and venturesome (Van den Brande)? The part played by the official Church varies according to the local situation. This is clear from the contributions dealing with a southern European concordat country (Italy; Bellini), a central European concordat country (the Federal Republic; Neumann), a country characterised by a complete separation between Church and State (France; Robert), an eastern European socialist country (Hungary; Hücking), young nations with a considerable number of Catholics (Africa; Heijke), a central American socialist country (Nicaragua; Cardenal) and a philosophically very mixed country (the Netherlands; van Ooijen). This factual survey closes with an analysis of the notorious 'Drinan affair' (Higgins).

PETER HUIZING
KNUT WALF

Translated by David Smith

Note

1. For this theme, we would point to Joseph A. Komonchak 'Clergy, Laity and the Church's Mission in the World' *The Jurist* 41 (1981) 2, 422-447.

PART I

The Political Role the Church Would Like to Play

Patrick Granfield

The Rise and Fall of
Societas Perfecta

'ALTHOUGH THE notion "People of God" is in itself best for explaining the social nature of the Church, it does not seem best for describing the Church *in actu*, because it does not explicitly convey the idea of *societas perfecta*. . . . The Church is a *societas perfecta* in the supernatural order, i.e., disposing all the means necessary to attain the supernatural end'.[1]

Karol Wojtyla, Bishop of Krakow, made these observations in an intervention at Vatican II. At first glance, they may appear out of harmony with the general ecclesiological tenor of the Council. However, it is significant that Wojtyla was from a communist country where there existed a strained relationship between Church and State. It seems reasonable to assume that it was more Wojtyla's personal political experiences than his theological principles that influenced his preference for the idea of *societas perfecta*.

As a designation for the Church, *societas perfecta* does not have a venerable history.[2] It is the product of the eighteenth and nineteenth centuries and was popular in theological circles from the time of Pius IX to that of Pius XII—a little over a century. To call a society 'perfect' does not refer to its excellence or holiness but rather to its self-sufficiency and autonomy. A perfect society, then, is one that is complete and independent in itself and possesses all the means necessary to attain its proposed end. To understand this idea more fully, it is useful to examine the context from which it arose, how it influenced ecclesiology, and how it is currently interpreted.

1. THE CHALLENGE

The classical distinction made by Pope Gelasius (d. 496) between temporal and spiritual authority was the basis for theories of Church-State relations for over a thousand years. In the middle ages the Church and State were not considered as two diverse, independent, or perfect societies, but rather two parts of a unified social reality—the *respublica christiana*. The *imperium* and *sacerdotium*, civil and ecclesiastical power, together formed the one perfect community, the Christian commonwealth.[3] The perennial and unresolved problem, of course, was the maintenance of balance between the two powers and the limits of authority each exercised. More often than not, there was an uneasy alliance with both sides complaining of interference.

Towards the end of the middle ages, the unitary view of society was gradually replaced by a dualistic concept. A major reason for this shift was the development of autonomous States and nations throughout Europe. Eventually, Church and State acted more or less as separate, self-governing realities. After the Reformation, however, other factors forced the Catholic Church to examine and clarify its relationship to secular governments.

First, there was the establishment of 'State churches' in Protestant parts of Europe. The principal theoretician of this idea was Samuel Pufendorf (d. 1694), a Protestant jurist. He proposed the 'Kollegialsystem' whereby the Church was seen as a *collegium* within the State. The Church was not independent and free to govern itself but was controlled by the State which was responsible for its external organisation. Pufendorf's view, later refined by Christopher Pfaff (d. 1760), was most influential, especially in Germany, in determining the relationship between civil and ecclesiastical power for several centuries. In effect, it permitted the government to interfere in the life of the Church.

Second, there were several movements that took place in the seventeenth, eighteenth and nineteenth centuries that were fundamentally political but caused severe repercussions in the Catholic Church. These included Gallicanism, Febronianism, Josephinism, the French Revolution, and the *Kulturkampf*. Although each of these had its own particular characteristics, all were motivated by a spirit of nationalism and all sought to restrict the authority of Rome over local churches and to increase the power of civil rulers in Church affairs. These movements threatened the freedom of the Catholic Church and forced it to react. It was out of the continuing confrontation between Church and State that the concept of *societas perfecta* was born.

Gallicanism, a seventeenth-century French version of conciliarism, attempted to limit the control of Rome over the French Church. The Four Gallican Articles, composed in 1682 by Bossuet, summarised its major tenets: complete independence of the French King from Roman control over temporal matters; the superiority of General Councils over the pope; the inviolability of the rights and customs of the Gallican Church; and the consent of the universal Church to validate papal judgments on faith and morals. Although several popes condemned Gallicanism, it was supported by many Catholics—bishops, priests, laity—throughout the eighteenth century.

Febronianism was named after Justinus Febronius, the pseudonym of Bishop von Hontheim (d. 1790), Auxiliary of Trier. In 1763, he published a book—put on the Index a year later—in which he advocated the creation of a national German Church that would be subject to the local ruler. Professedly nationalistic and antagonistic to Roman centralism, Febronianism condemned papal abuses, denied many of Rome's primatial claims, and advocated greater authority for bishops. Furthermore, like a kind of Gallicanism-across-the-Rhine, it taught that the Church and not the pope is infallible and that for any papal teaching to be irreformable it needs the consent of the universal Church or a General Council. Febronianism was most popular in German-speaking lands but it also had adherents in Portugal, Spain, the Netherlands, and parts of Italy.

Josephinism, the theory of Emperor Joseph II of Austria (d. 1790), attempted to subject the Church to the sovereign power of the State. Many religious orders were suppressed and Church property and finances were confiscated. The clergy were forbidden to correspond directly with the Holy See, the Emperor alone giving permission for papal decrees to be published. Episcopal sees and parishes were reorganised and clerical privileges reduced or abolished.

The French Revolution and the subsequent policies of Napoleon created a new political order that had a devastating effect on the Church of the nineteenth century. With nationalistic fervour, the government implemented a programme of de-Christianisation, secularisation, and anti-clericalism. The State, openly hostile to

Church authority, rejected traditional papal prerogatives, reorganised Church structures, expelled, imprisoned, or killed thousands of priests and religious, and expropriated religious property. The effects of these violent measures were most severely felt in France, but the Church also suffered greatly in Spain, Portugal, and parts of Germany. On the other hand, the events in France and their impact on the rest of Europe effectively weakened the influence and credibility of Gallicanism, Febronianism, and Josephinism.

The *Kulturkampf* (1871-90) initiated by Bismarck is our last example of harassment of the Church by the State. The civil authority appointed and dismissed the clergy, suppressed many religious orders (e.g., Jesuits, Redemptorists, Lazarists), exiled recalcitrant priests, and forbade communication with Rome. The Falk or May laws of 1873 gave the State control over seminary education and required that episcopal appointments be approved by the government. According to Bismarck's interpretation of Vatican I, the Pope 'has in theory replaced every individual bishop' and 'the bishops are now nothing but his tools, officials of a foreign sovereign'.[4] The repressive actions against the Church engendered by the *Kulturkampf* were not confined to Prussia; Austria, Switzerland, and other parts of Germany faced similar difficulties.

2. THE RESPONSE

The Catholic Church in Europe of the eighteenth and nineteenth centuries faced a widespread and virulent conflict with secular authorities. The problem was brought even closer to home with the increasing political unrest in Italy and the demands for civil emancipation within the Papal States. The Church's response to the entire situation was hampered by the decline in papal prestige and the inability to formulate an acceptable and unified view on the Church-State question.

Yet the Church did respond in a variety of ways. Several popes spoke out against any action of the State that threatened the *libertas ecclesiae*. Some problems were alleviated through concordats—about thirty in the nineteenth century—made between the Holy See and specific countries.[5] Another response, our concern here, was the development of the concept of *societas perfecta*. It was used by canonists, the *magisterium*, and theologians.

The Austrian canonist Franciscus Rautenstrauch (d. 1785) may have been the first to use the term. In a compilation of laws governing public debates during the reign of Maria Theresa, he wrote: 'The Christian society is of divine origin. It is a perfect society.'[6] In the following century, canonists like Taparelli (d. 1862), Tarquini (d. 1874), and Cavagnis (d. 1906) developed this idea. Treatises on public ecclesiastical law published up to the middle of this century commonly designated the Church as a *societas perfecta*. The canonists used the term to refute the Protestant jurists who held that the Church is not a perfect society but a *collegium* within the State. Furthermore, they insisted that both the Church and the State, each in its own order, is a perfect society. The canonists also argued that the proper power (*potestas propria*) of the Church is that which necessarily and essentially belongs to the Church as a perfect society.[7] The Code of Canon Law (1917) does not use the term *societas perfecta* but it is found in the first sentence of Benedict XV's *Providentissima mater ecclesia* promulgating the Code.[8]

The *magisterium* used the term frequently in the nineteenth century. One of the first times it is found in an official Roman document was in the 1839 response to the Gnesen-Posen debate over mixed-marriages in Prussia. Pius IX called the Church a perfect society in *Singulari quadam* (1854), *Multis gravibusque* (1860), *Maxima quidem laetitia* (1862), and *Vix dum a nobis* (1874). The concept was also a favourite with Leo XIII who used it in *Diuturnum illud* (1881), *Immortale Dei* (1885), *Sapientiae christianae*

(1890), and *Praeclara gratulationis* (1894). It was also employed on occasion by Pius X, Benedict XV, Pius XI, and Pius XII.

Vatican I did not use the notion of perfect society in *Pastor aeternus*. It did, however, appear as a central theme in the two major schemata on the Church—prepared for the Council but never publicly debated or voted on.[9] In *Supremi pastoris* we read: 'If anyone shall say that the Church is not a perfect society but a *collegium*, or that it is within civil society or the State in such a way that it is subject to secular power, let him be anathema.'[10] The other schema, *Tametsi Deus*, drafted by Joseph Kleutgen, also called the Church a perfect society and gave the following definition: 'A society, distinct from every other assembly of men, which moves towards its proper end and by its own ways and reasons, which is absolute, complete, and sufficient in itself to attain those things which pertain to it and which is neither subject to, joined as a part, or mixed and confused with any society.'[11]

Theologians, using papal documentation and the schemata of Vatican I, taught that Jesus founded the Church as a true, hierarchical, and monarchical society. This society, the Roman Catholic Church, is a perfect society, independent of every other society and endowed with all it requires to attain its end—the supernatural sanctification and salvation of humanity. A representative example of this approach is the manual of Joachim Salaverri. Writing a few years before Vatican II, he stated: 'The Church is a perfect society and absolutely independent, with full legislative, judicial, and coercive power.'[12] He attached the note 'De fide catholica' to this thesis as proposed by the universal and ordinary *magisterium* to be held (*tenenda*).

3. THE EFFECT ON ECCLESIOLOGY

The notion of perfect society fostered a juridical ecclesiology. The intense preoccupation with external and hierarchical elements obscured the understanding of the Church as mystery. Ecclesiology became, in Congar's phrase, 'hierarchology'. The impression was given that the Church as an organised society was distinct from the Church as a faith community of worship. Vatican II restored the view that the institutional and charismatic aspects of the Church are inseparable and together form 'one complex reality' (*Lumen gentium*, § 8).

There was also an ecumenical problem, since the true Church and the fully perfect society were equated. The Roman Catholic Church alone was the Church and all other Christian communities were 'non-churches'.[13] Vatican II, by recognising the presence of the Church of Christ in other churches and ecclesial communities, made ecumenical dialogue possible.

Finally, the perfect society ecclesiology did not provide for a theology of the local church. According to the manualists, local churches (dioceses) were not perfect societies, because they did not possess full legislative, judicial, and coercive power.[14] This overly universalist ecclesiology was corrected by Vatican II which taught that local churches are truly the Church. Karl Rahner notes that the concept of *societas perfecta* is inadequate to describe even the social and visible aspects of the Church, since it fails to acknowledge that the universal Church comes to be in the local church and that the Church is actualised in the local celebration of the Eucharist.[15]

4. THE CURRENT INTERPRETATION

The concept of *societas perfecta* developed as a theoretical construct to demonstrate the independence of the Church from unjustified civil interference. Although it began as a political expedient, it eventually was used to describe the essence of the Church. Today, theologians and canonists do not discuss Church-State relations in terms of two interacting perfect societies. There is no need, as R. Schwarz correctly observes, 'to continue using the concept of *societas perfecta*, because it carries too much of the burden of past history'.[16]

Vatican II did not use the term but preferred to speak of the Church as sacrament, People of God, Body of Christ, and as a prophetic, priestly, and eschatological community. At the same time, the Council preserved the basic elements of truth found in the idea of the perfect society.[17] Three aspects are significant.

First, the Council recognised the societal nature of the Church, even though it rarely used the term *societas* (e.g., *Lumen gentium*, § 8 and § 20; *Presbyterorum ordinis*, § 2). The social dimension of the Church was presented in the context of *communio*. The Church is a unique community—an assembly of faith, hope, and love in which all members with a variety of gifts and functions work together.

Second, Vatican II taught that the Church has all the means necessary to achieve its end. Through the presence of Christ in the Spirit, the means of salvation are available in the Word of God, the sacraments, virtues, and spiritual gifts (*Lumen gentium*, §11 *and* § 12; *Unitatis redintegratio*, § 3). Moreover, through a variety of ministries—exercised by bishops, priests, religious, and laity—the Church is able to fulfil its mission of proclaiming the Good News.

Third, the Council was unambiguous in insisting that the Church is different from the State and should have the freedom to carry on its mission without State interference. Governments, respecting the dignity of the human person, must allow religious bodies to govern themselves and not be hindered in the selection, training, and appointment of their ministers (*Dignitatis humanae*, § 1). Although the Church is not bound by any particular social, political, or economic system, it must encourage all that is true, good, and just in the world (*Gaudium et spes*, § 42 and § 44). Finally, in what is perhaps the closest parallel to the earlier idea of *societas perfecta*, we read: 'In their own proper spheres, the political community and the Church are mutually independent and self-governing' (*Gaudium et spes*, § 76).

In conclusion, the new ecclesiological perspective of Vatican II has made the concept of *societas perfecta* inappropriate. Today, we appeal to the basic principles of human dignity and religious liberty to vindicate the rights of the Church in a pluralistic world. The Church, of course, continues to insist on the right to preach the Gospel and to worship God in complete freedom without the control or hindrance of civil society. Only if this is granted can the Church reveal the full sacramental presence of Christ and be 'at once a sign and a safeguard of the transcendence of the human person' (*Gaudium et spes*, § 76).

Notes

1. *Acta synodalia* II, 3, 155-56.

2. See K. Walf 'Die katholische Kirche—eine "societas perfecta"?' *Theologische Quartals-chrift* 157 (1977) 107-118; M. Zimmermann *Structure sociale et église* (Strasbourg 1981).

3. See T. M. Parker 'The Medieval Origins of the Idea of the Church as a "Societas Perfecta" ' *Miscellanea historiae ecclesiasticae* (Stockholm Congress) (Louvain) 1961, pp. 23-31. St Thomas (*Summa theologiae*, 1a-2ae, q. 90, a.3, ad 3) calls the 'civitas' the perfect community, but according to T. Eschamnn, the perfect community for Thomas is the unity of both Church and State ('De societate in genere' *Angelicum* 11 [1934] 216).

B

4. For the response of the German bishops to Bismarck see Denzinger-Schönmetzer, 3112.

5. The concordats with Spain (1953) and the Dominican Republic (1954) explicitly mentioned that the two countries 'recognise in the Catholic Church the character of perfect society'.

6. *Synopsis iuris ecclesiastici publici et privati quod per terras haereditarias augustissimae Mariae Theresiae obtinet* (Vienna 1776) n. 31.

7. See J. Feiner 'Commentary on the Decree on Ecumenism' in *Commentary on the Documents of Vatican II* ed. H. Vorgrimmler (New York 1968), II: 69. (*Kommentar zum Dekret über den Ökumenismus* in *Lexikon für Theologie und Kirche. Das Zweite Vatikanische Konzil* [Freiburg-Basel-Wien, 1967], II: 50).

8. See U. Navarrete 'Potestas vicaria ecclesiae' *Periodica* 60 (1971) 415-486 and R. Schwarz 'De potestate propria ecclesiae' *Periodica* 63 (1974) 429-455.

9. See P. Granfield 'The Church as Societas Perfecta in the Schemata of Vatican I' *Church History* 48 (1979) 431-446.

10. Canon 10, Mansi, 51: 540.

11. Mansi, 53:315.

12. *Sacrae theologiae summa*, 3rd ed. (Madrid 1955), I: 826.

13. Many commentators, however, contend that the idea of perfect society is contained in Canon 100, § 1: 'The Catholic Church and the Apostolic See have the nature of a moral person by divine ordinance.'

14. See Y. Congar "Autonomie et pouvoir central dans l'Eglise' *Irénikon* 53 (1980) 298. He refers to Billot, Larcher-Schlagenhaufen, and Journet.

15. 'De praesentia Domini in communitate cultus' in *Acta congressus internationalis de theologia concilii Vaticani II* (Vatican 1968) p. 333.

16. R. Schwarz, in the article cited in note 8, 444.

17. Y. Congar discusses this question in 'Situation ecclésiologique au moment de "ecclesiam suam" given at the International Colloquium on *Ecclesiam suam*, Rome, 24-26 October 1980. To be published in the Acta of the Colloquium.

Raymond Lemieux

Priesthood and Politics: What Innocence?

QUESTIONS ABOUT the political involvement of the clergy are always overlaid, as it were, by an ideology of innocence, i.e., of being in a position to choose between purity and defilement, between the spiritual and the temporal, the Church and the world, God and Caesar. Yet history clearly shows the practical difficulties such innocence involves, since there is perhaps no historical problem more complicated than the relations between politics and religion. When one attempts to trace these relations through, at whatever period, one finds oneself faced with a skein of inextricably mingled strands. A first such strand is that of the relations between the two powers, endlessly refining the distinctions between the spiritual and the temporal; relations between areas of expertise, from the parish pulpit to the professorial chair, form another strand; another again, among the many remaining, is that of relations between visible institutions, from the Christian community to the whole community.

The visible Church has a history of its own; it produces members and gives them different roles; it inevitably therefore forms part of a political web, and so has political meaning. But how, today, does the Church speak about this aspect of itself? It cannot now, as Christendom did, harmonise Christian society and civil society, and make use of the secular arm *ad nutum et patentiam sacerdotis*. What are the areas of speech or silence that are still open to it? There is a growing awareness among Christians today that the end of Christian societies does not necessarily mean the end of Christianity (Delumeau 1977); that on the contrary, Christianity is perhaps learning to live freely again. However, the question of its relations to the political world is still unresolved. That being so, poverty and silence are as hazardous politically as speaking out. If, when it is freed of the bonds that may have tied its voice to that of the temporal power, a national hierarchy or any other religious grouping—the charismatics for example—entrenches itself in an attitude of political non-involvement, it is still making a statement. But what it is saying is unclear; it may be approving the authorities, or saying it has been rendered powerless to speak out. Since silence is open to any interpretation, it can often be a highly ambiguous policy. It fails to break the other's speech-flow and give any echo or feedback, and therefore becomes a meaningful element *within* what the other is saying. It may equally well attest or contest, but it can never be said to be politically meaningless.

As national States now cover the globe, the Church is subject wherever it exists to regimes which it does not control, even if it can still sometimes influence, or even dominate, their basic ideology. Like it or not, it is enmeshed in a web of action and discussion in which it takes part and by which it is therefore, often unwittingly, proportionately conditioned. Being itself a visible institution, the *assembly* of Christians, a bearer of values and ideals, with its own area of utterance—the expression of its faith—it occupies a place within society. Now, the political domain is simply the union or sum, represented by general and common aims (Dion 1971), of the existing places within a given social grouping. So like any other institution, the Church cannot avoid having the part it wants to play in society come under political control (Bergeron 1965). It has therefore to keep its political modes of being and thought under constant review.

1. THE QUESTION OF CHRISTIAN IDENTITY

Essentially, political statements by churchmen raise the problem of Christian identity and specifically Christian unity. When the boundaries of the Christian community and the political community cease to coincide, this problem becomes acute: by what right, and on what authority does a churchman make political statements? Does his right as a citizen confirm, or perfect, or endanger his right as a Church member? What is the nature of Christian identity, bound up as it is both with the visibility of an institution (which is of direct political concern) and with the mystery of its foundation (which concerns the Christian faith)?

This question is a thorn in the side of the Church. When it is either too close to the authorities or too critical of them, it is criticised for 'getting involved in politics'. When it stands back and remains uninvolved, it is criticised for not speaking out. Not surprisingly then, the question recurs time and again in the main pastoral documents of the last twenty years. *Lumen gentium* laid down the beginnings of a code of discipline in this regard: 'Because the human race today is joining more and more into a civic, economic, and social unity, it is that much more necessary that priests, united in concern and effort, under the leadership of the bishops and the Supreme Pontiff, wipe out every kind of division, so that the whole human race may be brought into the unity of the family of God' (ch. III, no. 28: *AAS* 57 (1965) 35).

From the start of his pontificate, John-Paul II has taken up and stressed this theme in his addresses to priests: 'The Christian people should be inspired to unity by the brotherly love and solidarity you show among yourselves (. . .). Leave political leadership to those whose responsibility it is; you yourselves have a different part, a magnificent part: you are leaders of a different kind and in a different way, since you share in the priesthood of Christ, as his ministers. Your sphere of action, and it is immense, is the sphere of faith and morals, in which you are expected to preach both by bold words and by living example' (John Paul II, a, 1980). 'You are close to all men and all their problems, "as priests"' (b, 1980).

When the thinking underlying these texts is examined, two arenas emerge, those of political identity ('civil, economic and social unity') and of Christian identity ('the unity of the family of God'). Christian identity is acted out *within* political identity, but the latter can endanger the former. The priest should therefore work first of all to strengthen Christian identity, an obligation which delimits the specific province of the priesthood, i.e., to be a sign of the Church in its unity and specific totality.

All human relations are based on some such form of identity; even at the most rudimentary linguistic level, it is only because one belongs somewhere, in some human grouping, that one can enter into relationship with another person. In the same way, perhaps, before the Church can speak politically, Christian identity has to exist; that is, the Church has to be occupying its own inalienable place in the concerted whole of existing social places. That is why texts like those quoted above are important politologically, and not just from the Church's internal and arbitrary disciplinary point of view. The questions these texts are now making aware Christians begin to ask concern the nature of Christian identity: in what way is the Christian community, as a *Christian* community, the locus of a *difference*, and how can this Christian identity express itself in an arena which is not the religious arena? Christendom as a historical system used in general to make unity of Church membership the basis of civil society. In those days, Christian identity was taken as a fact rather than a question, since the relations between the religious and the civil were defined in terms of suzerainty. But with the emergence of the double arena, the relation has been inverted, and the Church now has to search for and constantly affirm its specific being like any other institution.

This change has not caused the Church to cease labouring in the political arena; on the contrary, it sees it as a mission field, an area to be evangelised. Catholics have the duty to collaborate in this work. But the way this obligation is expressed in encyclicals and repeated on various occasions by national hierarchies reveals a twofold distinction: there is first the distinction, inherent in the Christian community, between the proper provinces of the priesthood and the laity; second, political activity as 'the politics of the common good', which determines the basic values of the civil community and so concern the whole Church, is distinguished from political activity as 'party politics'. 'By their specific ministry, bishops and priests bear witness to and are servants of the truth of the gospel and are the foundation of the unity of the people of God. That is why their task is to promote the evangelical values which should inspire all human activity, including politics; but they themselves, by reason of their mission, absolutely renounce any party political activity, direct or indirect, corporate or individual' (AEP 1980). The Puebla document makes the twofold distinction even clearer: 'The Church considers it has both the duty and the right to be present in this aspect of reality, since Christianity must evangelise every dimension of human existence, including the political dimension. So it criticises those who would confine faith to the realm of personal or family life, and exclude it from the professional, economic, social and political order, as if sin, love, prayer and forgiveness had no connection with it' (. . .). 'Pastors have great freedom of scope for evangelising the political arena without intervening in reserved areas'. However, 'by our very mission as promoters of unity, we, the clergy, have renounced any involvement in party politics. The party political is the province proper to the laity' (Puebla 1981).

The division into two areas of competence thus ratifies a distinction between two spheres of action, i.e., the political, and politics (nicely registered in French: *le* and *la* politique), a distinction which, it should be noted, itself derives from contemporary political science and is a foundation of modern political scholarship (Burdeau 1959). In the post-conciliar period, a doctrine seems to be being elaborated on the basis of this distinction, though as yet it is by no means definitive, and in some respects is still in its infancy, since it is both a theory of action and a testing ground for the theory: it aims at determining action and so is also, at least partly, determined by action. Inevitably so, for political knowledge can only be based on political practice. That is why some points are still unclear. The reader will remember how in Nicaragua, when priests who had accepted ministerial posts in the revolutionary government were subjected to pressure by their bishops to get them to give up these posts, they answered that 'they could see no conflict between loyalty to the Church and serving the poor in a revolutionary government' (APA 1981, 415). This kind of answer is not a refusal to comply, but merely points out the irrelevancy of the case being made; it accepts the discipline but considers it not applicable. For a revolutionary movement, pursuing the common good by definition involves overthrowing the existing regime, which in the end is a matter of party politics.

2. THE LEVELS OF CHURCH POLITICAL UTTERANCE

To develop our theme further, we now propose in our turn to distinguish between different levels of political utterance by the Church. In a given society, the mere fact that the Church operates in a certain way means that there exists in that society a concrete group with its own values, capable of sharing the values of the whole; the distinctions we are proposing seem to us therefore to be inherent in the very fact that the Church makes political statements. It should be pointed out that these distinctions are not based on a religious interpretation of the world of politics, but on a political interpretation of the religious world, or rather, to be precise, on a politological examination of its texts. From this point of view, three important levels stand out.

(a) Interest-group political utterance

Because the Church is a human collectivity in a given situation, and because the situation of the group always has political meaning, the Church has the same function as any other interest-group: defending its members when they come under attack because of their religious affiliation; promoting a form of social structure favourable to the way it sees its mission at a given moment of its history; claiming and holding certain rights, e.g., of expression, assembly or ownership; playing a part, out of its own locus, within the social institutions themselves: education, health, welfare, etc. At this level the interests of the Church are generally speaking those of its members seen from the point of view of their involvement in the life of the local community. We should note that the voice of the Church needs to be heard not only for the Church to function religiously, but also for the society to function politically. We shall therefore concentrate less on the content of the Church's utterances, which varies from one society to another, than on the form they take. At the political level, a society is a network of differing and mutually limiting interests; relative positions within the network are either negotiated or imposed, in recognition of and respect for the same law, or in a power game. To refuse to express one's own interests, to hide them, is to risk giving free play to political manipulators. That is why at this level even the choice of poverty or renunciation should be spelt out politically and should take into account the other interests it affects. This can be clearly seen when religious groups, for example, provide services without charging for their labour: they are probably undercutting paid workers and impeding the normal development of their interests. In other words they are probably playing into the hands of authorities which are themselves deaf and blind to possible demands from the workers. The Church may recognise that it has a religious duty to be poor, but politically it is not free to adopt whatever form of poverty it chooses.

Political utterances of this kind, from every level of the hierarchy, can easily be found. They are infrequent, however, in major pastoral documents like encyclicals or fundamental texts by episcopal assemblies, except in cases where the local churches are under threat from the regime or the status of their institutions is in jeopardy. In democratic countries with relatively stable institutions, this kind of utterance is probably made as and when the need arises, through a variety of social agents, in negotiations at a local level. It is nonetheless real. Furthermore, the Church's interests may not only be very diverse in themselves; they may also cover other interests if there are special groups such as ethnic or cultural minorities, age-groups, or particular socio-economic groupings within it. In economically advanced and other societies alike, the Church sometimes becomes the mouthpiece for disadvantaged minority groups which have become more or less unable to speak out for themselves, and it even offers these groups an alternative identity and means of social action. Far from being a more or less shameful compromise with the world, expression of interests can thus be for the Church a real and privileged form of service.

(b) Ethical utterance with a religious basis

The second level of political utterance by a Church in a situation shows the Church not as an interest group but as a locus for criticising and promoting general values which can direct social action. Basically, then, it puts forward an ethic, but because the ethic is developed from concrete situations, it has—at times immediate—political implications which must not be passed over without comment.

The most authoritative examples of this kind of utterance are doubtless the great encyclicals of the last twenty years. Once again it is obviously not possible to analyse their content here, but their structure deserves careful examination since it shows the manner in which the Church's most important political involvement occurs today. In general, these texts contain three main elements: a close and differentiated analysis of the situation; assertions of values, and finally a statement of the consequences pursuit of these values would have in organic political terms, i.e., as they would affect agents of social action, including States and the Church itself. The analysis of situations is of utmost importance in these documents. We should not forget that any situation is of relevance for evangelisation, whether it be ecological and demographic (exodus from the countryside, over-population, family), economic (related to labour and goods), social (inequalities between social strata) or even cultural (the right to be different, the social implications of technology, the conception of work, etc.). Obviously this kind of analysis does not write itself; its quality depends on the technical and intellectual tools available for producing it. It requires the Church to make use of real expertise which may be drawn if need be from non-members. The Church is dependent for these analyses on specialist knowledge which is not its exclusive property, and in all probability the effectiveness and authoritativeness of its utterance will depend, in part at least, on the general analytical resources it has available.

The manner in which the proclamation of values is made in these texts reveals a marked concern with effectiveness. It is adjusted according to the preoccupations of the moment and the particular sensitivities of the people the text is addressed to. In this respect it would be possible to draw differentiated portraits of the individual churches and the universal Church. Our analysis of statements by the Quebec assembly of bishops from 1963 to 1973, for example, demonstrated that the main values the assembly was concerned with were respect for freedom, responsibility, and national identity (Lemieux 1975); this complex of themes obviously reflects a particular politico-social context. Similarly, one could show how encyclicals from *Mater et Magistra* to *Laborem Exercens* portray the universal Church as being sensitive to the questions of the day: the right to a decent way of life; development; respect for life; the right to worker participation and to a proper return for labour, etc. The proclamation of such values normally leads in these texts into a view of the functions of the State: defending the weak; promoting development; regulating the division of labour; and arbitrating in cases of conflict. State structures themselves, however, are only touched on exceptionally, if they directly conflict with the values themselves. The Church can provide objectives and may go so far as to suggest means of action and on occasion even strategies, but it has no models of government to recommend. Rather it recognises that the structure of the State, both at the supra-national and world level and at the national level, must be *sui generis*.

(c) Theological utterance

There is a third level of utterance, which is rarely perceived as political, but which nevertheless has political effects since it is directly related to Christian identity. It is *theological* in the sense that it involves seeking out the foundations, in the gospel and tradition, of the values promulgated by the Church. The proclamation of universal values does not in itself put in question Christian identity; on the contrary, the concern for political effectiveness implies rather that when the Church proclaims universal values it is seeking agreement between itself and other social agents with different starting-points. Ethics are not peculiar to Christianity; rather, they are an entitlement to speak out, that is, to make possible some desirable quality of life. That is why if the Church is visibly to occupy a meaningful and inalienable place within the overall network of particular group interests and values that have to be defended, it must continually make an effort to assert the reality of its mystery. It can only truly represent a *different* locus if it makes this effort. That is what we mean by the theological level of utterance which, because of its social effects, is nonetheless political. It is the locus of the Church's specific difference and fundamental otherness.

This otherness cannot be defined by reference to a politological interpretation of the texts such as we are now engaged in. It must be stated, however, because this otherness is the reason why, seen from the Church's locus—which cannot be reduced to its historically identifiable social identity—no value and no utterance can be taken as definitive. The theological level of the Church's utterance, since it witnesses to an otherness, can never be satisfied with an object which is not this otherness. So any social order, any concrete network of values, any ideology and any human achievement are, for theological utterance, relative, that is to say, potentially open to criticism. The absolute is elsewhere.

Basically, perhaps the essential political message of the Church is precisely this refusal to recognise the political as an absolute. That is why its utterances are so pervaded by the problematical question of Christian identity. Indeed, can Christian identity be other than problematical, when it is lived out in time and place? If it were not so, the very words the Church uses, with all their historical relativity, would acquire absolute value. So the Church's utterances about politics have of necessity to make a divide within the historical arena, not from a basis of knowledge of man and the world, which is a shared knowledge, but from a basis of non-knowledge about Christian identity. They introduce into the historical arena an unpredictable otherness which divides political utterance: the whole political area must be evangelised but not all political commitment is possible; a Catholic must labour in the political field but one who represents the Church must avoid partisan commitment.

Translated by Ruth Murphy

References

AEP (Assemblée des évêques du Pérou) 'Les Chrétiens et la politique' *Documentation Catholique* (1980) pp. 961-962.
APA (Agencia prensa asociada) 'La Participation de prêtres au gouvernement' *Documentation Catholique* (1981) p. 415.
Bergeron, G. *Fonctionnement de l'Etat* (Paris 1965).
Burdeau, G. *Traité de science politique* (Paris 1959).
Delumeau, J. *Le Christianisme va-t-il mourir?* (Paris 1977).
Dion, L. *Société et politique: la vie des groupes* (Quebec 1971)
Jean Paul II (*a*) 'Discours aux prêtres du Zaïre' *Documentation Catholique* (1980) pp. 512-515. (*b*) 'Discours aux prêtres de France' *Documentation Catholique* (1980) pp. 558-561.
Lemieux, R. 'Discours politiques et légitimités religieuses' *Changement social et religion*. Actes de la 13e Conférence internationale de sociologie religieuse, Lloret de Mar, 31 août-4 sept. 1975 (Lille).

Albert Gnägi

The Constitution of the Church and Patterns of the State

A TIGHT-ROPE walk between principle and opportunism.

Anyone who tries to discover what the relationship between the Catholic Church and the different political constitutions really is, will find that the authoritative texts on the subject leave him in more confusion than when he began. For one thing, there are too many contradictory approaches, so that the inquirer is finally left at a loss—unless, indeed, he puts aside everything that the popes have said on the subject during the last hundred years (not to mention theologians even earlier) and contents himself with the texts of the Second Vatican Council, especially the Declaration on Religious Liberty and the famous No. 76 of the Pastoral Constitution on the Church in the World of Today, *Gaudium et spes*.

Another difficulty, however, is that there is a quite evident contradiction between the Church's theory and its practice. Theoretically it claims to be neutral towards the different political forms. In practice it has a preference for particular types of constitution, because the Church's hierarchy could—and still can—get along with them more easily than with the others. It must be added at once, however, that a great deal has changed here in recent years and decades; and today's more differentiated state of affairs cannot be summed up under any single, slickly shallow formula.

The Austrian constitutionalist Hans Kelsen once wrote that every political viewpoint has its corresponding philosophy. If we reverse this axiom, we could well assume that the Catholic Church pays homage to a particular political system, not merely in fact but even in principle. It is apparent that, right down to the present day, many contemporaries have seen the behaviour of the Catholic Church as confirmation of this assumption. And the political view which was considered to be the counterpart of the Catholic philosophy of life was certainly not democracy. Arnold Toynbee once maintained that 'Some of the most high-handedly revolutionary apostles of "the totalitarian state"—from a Habsburg Joseph II and a Corsican Napoleon I to a Romagnol Mussolini and an Upper Austrian Hitler—are the nurslings of purely Catholic environments' (*A Study of History* (London 1939) IV p. 219). And Toynbee is only one prominent voice among the whole chorus of those who claim that the Catholic Church is fundamentally incapable of democracy, and that it has a special affinity—indeed an essential one—with authoritarian regimes.

15

The reproach is really a remarkable one; for practically ever since the rise of democracy and the modern constitutional State, a whole series of important statements have been made by the Church and the popes affirming fundamental neutrality towards the different constitutional forms. Leo XIII, for example, writes in his apostolic letter *Au milieu des sollicitudes* (1892): 'Where this purely theoretical discussion is in question, Catholics, like every other citizen, are completely free to give preference to one form of government rather than another. This is so for the very reason that none of these forms of society *per se* stands in contradiction to the pronouncements of sound reason or the principles of Christian doctrine.' After this avowed neutrality had been repeatedly stressed by the popes who succeeded Leo XIII, the Second Vatican Council confirmed on 7 December 1965, in *Gaudium et spes* that the Church was not bound to any one political system (No. 76). This avowal of neutrality is irrelevant, however, as long as other ecclesiastical statements call in question the essential foundations of a particular political form. For example, neutrality towards the democratic form of the State is a hollow mockery as long as the Church denies democracy's fundamental principle, which is popular sovereignty; or as long as it imposes on the State a duty to safeguard the truth (which in the Church's eyes has to be one and the same as its own doctrine), even though this duty is incompatible with the democratic principle of freedom of faith and conscience, or with the compromise which democracy's political institutions embody.

This means that if we want to arrive at further clarity about the Church's attitude to the various constitutional forms, we ought not to content ourselves, in our investigation, with the verbal assurance of fundamental neutrality. We ought really to consider the attitude of the Church to the fundamental statements of the different political forms. But this would go beyond the scope of this essay.

Let us confine ourselves here to the question: how does a constitutional democracy or a modern constitutional State differ from an authoritative or totalitarian regime? And where does the Church's doctrine and constitution belong, in the framework of this distinction.

1. POPULAR SOVEREIGNTY

In a constitutional democracy, the processes of government are built up from below to above. The people sustain the power of the State, and generally appoint at periodical intervals the persons who are to exercise this power. In the authoritarian or totalitarian regime this possibility does not exist, or only exists nominally. The person who governs the State (who has often achieved power by irregular means) is either 'elected' for life; or declares that the people are not yet mature enough to vote; or holds elections which have nothing in common with what are usually termed free elections, either in the way they are prepared, or in the way they are carried out, or as regards the candidates standing for election. The processes of government are exercised from the top downwards.

2. THE CONTROL OF POWER AND THE PRINCIPLE OF LEGALITY

Constitutional democracy incorporates a whole series of checks and balances which are designed to prevent the power of the State from becoming absolute, or from being concentrated unduly and without restriction in a single hand. The main security is the separation of powers. In an authoritarian or totalitarian regime, on the other hand, there is generally no effective separation of powers. Parliament has either been dissolved, or changed into a body for pure acclamation. The courts are not independent. They are either subject to directives, or are presided over by appropriately obsequious puppets.

In a constitutional democracy legislature, executive and judiciary are subject to law; and even the legislature has to adhere in what it does to the formal rules of legislative process (the principle of legality). In the case of an arbitrary intervention by the State, or acts of State that do not rest on an adequate legal basis, redress can usually be sought in the courts by the person concerned; and the said acts may be declared null and void if the circumstances warrant it. In an authoritarian or totalitarian regime, on the other hand, government is frequently or generally exercised by decree, emergency powers and martial law, under the pretext of a state of emergency, or whatever the suspension of the constitution may be called. The right of the person affected to take legal action is generally illusory.

3. HUMAN RIGHTS AS SAFEGUARD OF A SPHERE FREE FROM GOVERNMENTAL CONTROL

The citizen belonging to a constitutional democracy has a free space in which the State is not permitted to interfere and which is none of the State's business. Human rights help to safeguard this sphere. And indeed when they first came into being, human rights were interpreted as rights *against* the State. These fundamental human rights, which are designed to guarantee liberty from the State, include freedom of religion, freedom of opinion, freedom of association and demonstration, and the right to the due process of law. Ever since the Virginia Declaration of Rights (1776) and the declaration of human rights made at the French Revolution, the catalogue of these rights has been expanded and further differentiated. The essential points about them are the assertion of equality, the prohibition of despotism, the claim to a just hearing, etc. In the authoritarian or totalitarian regime important parts of this catalogue are frequently abolished or considerably restricted, or are reduced in actual practice to a farce.

In what follows we shall be asking what Church doctrine has to say about these things, and shall also be examining the Church's constitution, in order to see whether it is closer to the pattern of a constitutional democracy, or to the authoritarian-totalitarian pattern. This is not as yet the same thing as a demand for, let us say, the introduction of popular sovereignty into the Church. But we can surely ask whether the specific form of centralism existing in the Church, or certain characteristics of ecclesiastical jurisdiction, for example, are unalterable *ius divinum*; or whether these and other sore spots are not really determined to a large extent by historical contingency and chance.

4. THE CHURCH AND POPULAR SOVEREIGNTY

There is no need to stress the fact that popular sovereignty is a principle that is diametrically opposed to the constitution of the Roman Church. The Church's processes of government move from above downwards, its office-bearers are appointed from above downwards, and even where—as in Switzerland, for example—the parish priest may in certain places be chosen by the people, or where laymen are conceded certain rights in the appointment of office-holders, on the basis of ancient rights of patronage, this applies only to the person's *nomination*. Once appointed, he receives the authority to exercise his office from above, on the basis of canon law.

The Church also has a highly ambiguous relationship to popular sovereignty as a principle of *civil* government. Historically speaking, this has often been dictated by opportunism. For example, when the middle ages were at their height, the Church's interests were quite different from what they were in the nineteenth century. During the conflicts between the Holy Roman Emperor and the pope, the Church's aim was to strengthen the sovereign power of individual kings and princes, as a bastion against the claims of the Emperor. So it is not surprising that in the middle ages the rights of the people and strivings for independence—and hence popular sovereignty—were judged in a kindly and benevolent light by the Church too. For at that time this intensification of regional powers was an ecclesiastical weapon against the pope's antagonist, the Emperor.

In the nineteenth century things were very different. At this time strivings for independence and revolutionary movements often went hand in hand with anti-clericalism, hostility towards the Church and actual persecution. Accordingly the *magisterium* found it hard to come to terms with popular sovereignty. Even though Boniface VIII's theory of the Two Swords, and with it the supremacy of Church over State, was no longer defended with any special emphasis, yet there was still a continual appeal to Romans 13. Paul's assertion that God was the author of all authority, and the command to obedience which went along with this, was consistently interpreted as meaning that princes and kings took their authority directly from God, and that revolutions were therefore a rebellion against him. Even Leo XIII still found it difficult to come to terms with popular sovereignty: according to him, popular elections could merely designate the people who were to hold office (the designation theory); they could not actually confer authority on them. In this way they resembled the rights of patronage in the Church.

It was only when the question had become obsolete (because there were practically no ruling princes in Europe any longer) that the *magisterium* accepted the principle of popular sovereignty. In an address to the Sacra Romana Rota in 1945 Pius XII formulated the matter as follows: 'If, on the other hand, we remember democracy's main postulate—that the original upholder of the God-given authority of the State is the people (not , incidentally, "the masses")—a thesis which excellent Christian thinkers have maintained at all periods—then the difference between Church and State, even the democratic State, becomes increasingly clear' (*Acta Apostolica Sedis* 37 (1945) 259).

5. THE CONTROL OF POWER—A PRINCIPLE ALIEN TO ECCLESIASTICAL THINKING

According to canon law, the pope unites in his person the fullness of legislative, judicial and executive power in the Church. The contrast with the constitutional principle that power should be subject to control could not well be greater. So it is not surprising that this influenced the Church's doctrine of the State. Thomas Aquinas, who followed Aristotle closely at this point, started from the assumption that human society, like every other organism, requires a unifying principle if it is to be capable of living and functioning. The greater the unity, the better it functions, and the better the State can fulfil its purpose, which is to ensure the common good. But the greatest unity is to be found in the rule of a single individual—the king; and the monarchy is therefore theoretically the best form of government. As late as 1945 Cardinal Journet said exactly the same thing in his book *Exigences chrétiennes en politique* (Paris 1945); though the monarchy he means is not of course identical with an authoritarian or totalitarian regime. None the less, this value-judgment shows clearly that the quality of a government was seen as depending mainly on its theoretical potentiality for realising the common good efficiently—which meant quickly and, if possible, without discussion. The possibility that an 'efficient' government of this kind can *endanger* the common good equally effectively was certainly not overlooked; but it mainly provided the occasion for reminding the heads of government of the divine judgment. Leo XIII did this repeatedly. The notion that the subjective co-operation and assent of the citizens concerned could also contribute to the specific realisation of the common good appears to be alien to thinking of this kind.

The *principle of legality* seems to raise the fewest difficulties. Judicial structures are anything but alien to the Church, and canon law, in all its ramifications, is not without obligation for people holding office in the Church at least, even if wider circles today regard it as a dead letter, and even though the legal protection which the Church provides is in a poor way.

6. THE CRUX: HUMAN RIGHTS, AND ESPECIALLY RELIGIOUS LIBERTY

The value attached to human rights, and especially religious liberty, is one of the most impressive examples of a change in the Church's attitude. At the beginning of the nineteenth century Gregory XVI still branded the idea of religious liberty as madness; it was condemned in the Syllabus of 1864; Pius XII still declared it to be merely tolerable in certain situations, as the lesser evil; and it was only in 1965 that the Vatican Council solemnly proclaimed it to be a fundamental right rooted in the nature of man. Seldom has a change of mind been so strikingly evident. Right down to the middle of the twentieth century, the doctrine of the Church failed to grasp that in a political society it is only people, not ideas, that enjoy rights. As a theological or philosophical axiom, it may perhaps be correct that an error has no right to exist. But this maxim was turned into a principle of political behaviour, so that the State had imposed upon it the duty to promote the one true religion. It was quite consistent for non-Catholic countries to be enjoined to grant religious liberty to Catholics; and equally consistent when Catholic States were exhorted not to concede the same freedom to non-Catholics, or at least only to a very limited degree (tolerance for the sake of avoiding a still greater evil).

We find the same attitude towards most of the other human rights as well. For example, in his encyclical *Libertas praestantissimum* (1888) Leo XIII did not condemn freedom of speech and liberty of the press as such, but he did condemn its distortion: 'It is right that the authority of the laws should suppress the errors of a wanton spirit, which are truly an act of violence committed against the inexperienced people, just as they suppress an injustice committed against the weak by open violence.' Here it is presupposed quite as a matter of course that the State knows what justice and injustice is, what is right and what wrong, what truth and what error. The parellels with an authoritarian or totalitarian regime leap to the eye. We may think especially of Communist countries which, though paying lip-service to human rights and though signatories of the Helsinki agreement, are not thereby prevented from allowing freedom of the press to come to grief because of shortage of paper (not to mention more drastic sanctions); the aim being to prevent, not only the Church's publications, but also the dissemination of 'errors' or deviations from 'the true Leninist doctrine'.

Under John XXIII the Catholic Church completed its about-turn and said good-bye to the age of Constantine, which imposed on the State a task for which—according to our interpretation today—it is not suited. The doctrine of the Church, at least in its official texts, has won through to the insight that the modern contemporary State is neutral in its philosophy of life. It therefore cannot be its function to grant privileges to the Catholic Church. Special rights conceded through concordats or in other ways can be a cause of offence, and must if necessary be given up (*Gaudium et spes*, No. 76). At the same time the picture of the citizen belonging to this modern State changed too. He ceased to be an object to be protected and became the subject of rights. Instead of being subordinate to his governors, and in need of guidance, he became someone possessed of certain rights as a human being. This *Copernican revolution in the Catholic view of the*

State and its citizens is only a few decades old. It should be no surprise to anyone who recognises the force of history and comprehends the burden of tradition that the Church needs time to accustom itself in actual practice to the new state of affairs; and that dissociation from the authoritarian State is not always and everywhere found easy. The implications for the internal practice of the Church where human rights are concerned (the due process of law, or the right to a proper hearing) should be obvious enough.

Translated by Margaret Kohl

Jean-Marie Mayeur

Catholic Parties, Christian Democratic Parties and the Catholic Church

ALONGSIDE CONSERVATIVE or traditionalist right-wing parties, liberal, demo-cractic and radical parties, socialist and communist parties, the Catholic and Christian Democratic parties represent one element of the political landscape of Europe in the nineteenth and twentieth centuries. Their influence has extended into Latin America in our own century. All these parties are, or were for a very long time, 'religious' parties, proclaiming, in various ways, their allegiance to a particular Church or to Christian principles. This article seeks, from an historical standpoint, to formulate some thoughts concerning the relations of these parties with the Catholic Church, which have been more complex than is sometimes imagined.

In order to throw some light on this subject, perhaps one should begin with some definitions. If the term Christian Democratic parties should create no difficulties, the notion of Catholic parties might be challenged as imprecise or even polemical. It might, rightly, be pointed out that in fact the German Centre Party refused any denominational label and that Windthorst continually insisted on this point. However, there are several reasons, which are not merely matters of convenience, which favour the use of the term Catholic party. It has the great merit of encompassing a reality which is wider and more diverse than that covered by the term Christian Democratic party, which only acquired its significance gradually and would be inappropriate to the Belgian or Dutch Catholic parties, for example. A comparative analysis cannot be restricted merely to the Christian Democrats, which are in fact components of a larger whole.

The term Catholic party was employed, at the time, not only by the opponents of such parties but frequently by their leaders themselves. If the German Centre Party had no denominational label, the *Katholische Volkspartei* (Catholic People's Party), which came into existence in the Grand Duchy of Baden at the end of the 1860s, openly proclaimed its denominational allegiance. In short, although the term Catholic party was not always employed, and though it was sometimes rejected by these political groups, it is nevertheless true that it is the most accurate expression of what happened in practice, as it was experienced by contemporaries and as it must be recognised by the historian. Thus it may seem legitimate to have recourse to the term Catholic party, which is in fact particularly appropriate in the nineteenth century, whereas the rise of

21

the Christian Democratic parties belongs more properly to the twentieth.

To be exact, the terms Christian Democratic and Catholic parties by no means exhaust all the different names which have been used. Federation of Catholic Societies in Belgium, Catholic People's Party (in the Netherlands, in Baden and in Hungary in 1894), Centre Party, People's Democratic Party, Democratic League (as in Belgium in 1891), Federation of Democratic Republicans (in France just before the Great War), M.R.P. (Popular Republican Movement): this list of party names, which is probably incomplete, provides sufficient grounds for comments and questions. Denominational labels are relatively infrequent amongst such titles. Parties more often preferred some reference to Christianity, as being interdenominational and likely to appeal to Protestants, or even to unbelievers who felt some attachment to Christian morality, and as indicating their independence of action with regard to the Catholic hierarchy.

Non-denominationalism was, even before 1914, the policy of the German Centre, but also, for example, of the *Schweizerischer Konservative Volkspartei* (Swiss Conservative People's Party) founded in 1912, or of the Right-wing Party in Luxembourg, founded on 9 January 1914. The programme of these non-denominational parties claimed, however, to be based on the 'Christian view of the world' and 'Christian social policies'. The diversity and the evolution of party names deserve attention: direct reference to Christianity appears in Germany and Italy only after the Second World War. In Austria, on the other hand, it was a non-denominational title which succeeded the Christian Social label in 1945 with the *Österreichischer Volkspartei* (Austrian People's Party).

The study of Catholic and Christian Democratic parties over more than a century and a half of history cuts across two other areas of study which are closely related but distinct: the Catholic Church and politics, and Catholics and politics. The relationship between the Church and politics was not confined to the medium of the parties. For many years, moreover, the Church preferred to work through approaches made by the bishops and the Curia to a head of State, the successor of the 'Christian prince', rather than the activities of parliamentary parties controlled by laymen. Few images could be more inaccurate than the one which represents Catholic or Christian Democratic parties as the 'secular arm' of the hierarchy or the Holy See. At the time of the settlement of the *Kulturkampf*, Rome negotiated directly with Bismarck without paying any heed to the Centre Party. In 1943, the Curia felt little enthusiasm for the foundation of a great Christian Democratic party in Italy. Again, rather than action through parties, the Church preferred to work through Catholic organisations, acting as pressure groups on those in power and on the various parties concerned with the defence of Catholic interests, such as, in France, the Catholic National Federation in 1924, or the Parliamentary Association for Educational Freedom in 1951. The scope of the relations between the Church and politics extends, then, beyond the Catholic parties.

It is equally impossible to confine the study of the political attitudes of Catholics to the destiny of Catholic parties, although it is indispensable to the understanding of their history. In Great Britain the Catholics, comprising a minority of the population, have never formed a political party, unlike those in another country where they are a minority, the Netherlands. In France and Spain, countries where Catholicism is the majority religion, Catholic or Christian-based parties have only had a brief existence and a mediocre fate. These failures are indications of the pluralism of the political behaviour of Catholics and of their reluctance to accept the formula which was to attain, in the German-speaking world and, albeit belatedly, in Italy, a remarkable degree of success. It must nevertheless be pointed out that, even in the heyday of the Centre Party, not all German Catholics voted for the party of Windthorst. As the memory of the battles of the *Kulturkampf* faded, this phenomenon became more marked.

When seeking a strict definition of those parties which proclaimed at the very moment of their foundation their allegiance to Catholicism and Christian principles it is not possible to include dynastic or conservative parties within the category of Catholic parties, even when they included numerous Catholics and gave a considerable place in their programme to the defence of religion. Neither Carlism in Spain nor Legitimism in France qualify for inclusion. Their founding principle was fidelity to a dynasty, even if their loyalty to God and their attachment to the king were one and the same. Similarly, conservative groups, like the Party of Order in the France of the Second Republic, or the Republican Federation between the wars, do not merit the appelation Catholic parties. They grouped around a programme which was primarily political men who, in certain cases, like Thiers or Louis Marin in France, had no particular links with the Church. Concern for the defence of the 'interests of religion' and the presence of numerous Catholics amongst their supporters were not sufficient to turn them into Catholic parties.

The conditions which favoured the emergence of Catholic and Christian Democratic parties constitute a first group of problems. The existence of a parliament and a representative system was one precondition. Then parliamentary groups, such as the Prussian Centre in 1852, began to develop, accompanied by certain tendencies in public opinion, if not actual organised parties. Another precondition relevant here was the existence of a State which was 'indifferent in matters of religion', in La Mennais's phrase. In a Catholic monarchy or a Christian State the idea of a party proclaiming allegiance to Catholicism would obviously be absurd. On the other hand, as soon as Catholicism was no longer the State religion, but merely the 'dominant' religion, as was decreed by the concordat in France, for example, and as secularisation developed, Catholics, or at least a section of them, aspired to the exercise of liberal institutions and appealed to public opinion. Montalembert's 'Catholic party' provides a useful example of this process. In the Netherlands and in Prussia the presence of a Protestant ruler produced the same consequences.

Not only the form of the relationship between Church and State, but also the geographical distribution of religious groups affected the establishment of Catholic parties. Indisputably they achieved their first successes in those States in which Catholicism was a minority religion, and they appeared as the necessary means of defending the rights of Catholics, who were confined to a position of inferiority. O'Connell's Catholic Association in Ireland, the early political activites of Catholics in Prussia, the activities of Belgian Catholics in the Kingdom of the Netherlands, provide examples of this phenomenon. It must also be noted that these Catholic minorities were in fact in the majority within a given geographical entity, the Rhineland, Ireland and what was to become Belgium. The religious map of Europe, drawn up in the late sixteenth century, at the time of the Reformation, according to the principle *cuius regio, eius religio* which compelled subjects to accept the religion of their sovereign, still exerts an influence today on the geography of political parties. For many years the Bavarian CSU enjoyed its greatest success in those regions where a long Catholic tradition had persisted from the sixteenth century.

It is obviously true that Catholic parties did not come into existence only in States where Catholicism had minority status but, at their origin, one always discovers the desire to fight against the anticlerical policies of the liberals in power, which turned Catholics into second-class citizens. The Italian Popular Party sought to recover for Catholics their place in the political system. In the Austrian Empire, another State in which Catholics were in the majority, the Christian Social Party, at the end of the nineteenth century, sought to end the dominant influence of the liberals.

These were, then, originally, parties devoted to the defence of religion, concerned to ensure the protection of the rights of the Church in the domain of common law. But they

c

acquired, with varying degrees of urgency, a political and social programme in the true sense, based on a political and social philosophy and a conception of the State which were Christian in inspiration. It is not certain that parties concerned simply with defending religion would have been able to endure. However, their affirmation of the conception of man and the world proclaimed in the political and social teaching of the Church gained for these parties the support, although it was not always consistent and wholehearted, of the hierarchy and the clergy. It formed the basis of their strength and their continuity. Above all, these parties discovered a breeding-ground of activists and a devoted team of workers in the charitable bodies and associations of so many kinds which developed in a particularly remarkable way from the end of the nineteenth century onwards, foreshadowing the rise of Catholic Action. The latter has trained a large number of activists, whose political commitment was expressed in the ranks of Catholic and Christian Democratic parties.

It is frequently stated nowadays that the Catholic parties sprang up in the traditional regions of Christendom, those in which, even today, the practice of Christianity is particularly fervent. In fact, the religious vitality of a region, although a necessary condition, was not sufficient to produce a Catholic party. It was no less indispensable that there should exist a network of associations and movements which enclosed the population in that *Vereinskatholizimus* (Catholic community) which played an essential part in the history of German Catholicism but which, in Venetia as in Flanders or Slovakia, enjoyed a no less remarkable destiny. Thus the Catholic parties were indeed the political expression of a 'popular' Catholicism, deeply rooted in its local soil—in short, of a 'social' Catholicism. They became one element of the landscape of Christendom, like the charitable bodies, the associations, the Christian trades unions, whether agricultural or industrial.

The Catholic parties were born out of the reaction against anticlerical policies and the conviction of militant Catholics that they were being excluded from a political life dominated by the liberals. When Don Sturzo founded, in 1919, the Italian Popular Party, he wished, profiting from the lifting of the *non-expedit* (the papal prohibition of Catholic participation in elections), to reject the 'clerico moderato' agreement of 1913 and to affirm uncompromisingly the autonomy of the Catholic elements in society. He was just as hostile to a compromise with the bourgeois ruling class as to an alliance with socialism. The birth of his PPI was indeed the culmination of the long struggle of Italian Catholics against the liberal State. Liberal and anticlerical policies favoured the coming into existence of Catholic parties.

As parties concerned simply with defending religion, these parties could have confined themselves to protecting the rights of Catholics in the domain of common liberties which Catholics, like all other citizens, should enjoy. This was one of the lines of argument followed by Windthorst at the time of the *Kulturkampf*. But from a 'defensive' political Catholicism they went over to a 'proselytising' political Catholicism, concerned with ensuring for the Church a privileged religious position, by passing laws which would create a favourable climate for religious life, particularly where education was concerned, as in Belgium from 1884 onwards.

Finally, beyond simple proselytism, it was sometimes possible to discern the concept of a 'theocratic' political Catholicism, in parliamentary form. Such was the view of Catholic parties formulated by their opponents and expressed with admirable clarity by the Belgian liberal, Emile de Laveleye: '*In the middle ages, popes sought to deprive kings of their crowns by excommunicating them: they almost never succeeded. Today a command is sent forth from Rome; it is passed on by bishops and parish priests; the electors obey, and thus, by means of the ballot-box, the Supreme Pontiff appoints or dismisses ministers and governs States.*' This was a theme which was endlessly repeated:

the Catholic parties appeared to their opponents to be the latest stratagem of theocracy. Doubtless, the reality was more complex. The fact remains that the theocratic dream was never totally absent: one may recall the attitude of Fornari, nuncio in Brussels just after independence, or the hopes of certain Italian Christian Democrats, loyal to a 'Guelph' tradition which persisted until the time of Dossetti or La Pira, with the dream of a new Christendom.

In fact, throughout their history, the Catholic parties experienced, not without contradictions and difficulties, the ambiguous condition which stemmed from their very nature, from their close relations with the bishops, the clergy, the Catholic organisations, and also with their electorate. Denominationalism, interdenominationalism with Protestants, non-denominationalism, the limitations of political autonomy with regard to the Church, relations with the hierarchy and Rome—so many subjects of controversy, conflicts and even divisions. Party labels referring to Catholicism were, in fact, less frequent than the interdenominational reference to Christianity which was the basis for Windthorst's appeal for collaboration with Protestants or even unbelievers. It is no doubt true that Protestant participation in the Centre remained small. It did, however, increase during the last years of the Weimar Republic, foreshadowing the co-operation which was later established within the CDU.

Their Christian basis did not mean, for Catholic and Christian Democratic parties, any renunciation of political autonomy in relation to the hierarchy. It meant, above all, adherence to a political and social morality. Nevertheless, the risk of ambiguity led to calls for non-denominationalism: the Popular Democratic Party founded in France in 1924, like the PPI in 1919, affirmed this vigorously. The German Centre itself unceasingly proclaimed that it was not a denominational party. Moreover, unlike the *Christliche Demokratische Union* founded just after the Second World War, its name contained no explicit reference to Christianity.

Relations which were more complex than is often stated were established between the leaders and activists of these parties and the religious authorities. The hierarchy, in Italy, Belgium, Germany and the Netherlands, until just a few years ago, regularly declared, on the eve of elections, its support for the Catholic parties. In practice, their links with the religious authorities were therefore close. But within this situation the Catholic parties preserved a freedom of action which must be assessed in the light of different national situations, and of the absence of homogeneity, or even divisions, amongst the bishops. As early as the end of the last century, the historian Charles Seignobos foresaw that between the laity and the 'official leaders of the Church', 'rivalries for influence and differences of opinion' would provoke 'conflicts of a new kind'. Already Montalembert's 'Catholic party' in 1846—in reality a pressure group for freedom of education—had aroused suspicion amongst one section of the bishops, who were concerned about 'laicism'. New authorities were extending their influence over the minds of the faithful. Political struggles could only divide Catholics. Was it not better to deal directly with governments without using a political party as an intermediary? Such were very often the arguments of the bishops, attached to the traditional image of the relations between Church and State.

At times their reservations became open hostility, when Catholic parties adopted a social programme which aroused the opposition of conservative Catholics, and when a section of the younger clergy participated actively in these parties despite the wishes of the hierarchy. The suspicions of the upper clergy of the Austrian Empire concerning the *Kaplansbewegung* (Curates' Movement) are well known: their complaints to Rome, based notably on the combined anti-capitalism and anti-semitism of the Christian Social Party, and the support given to the latter by Cardinals Agliardi and Rampolla. In that case, Rome seemed to support a Catholic party over the heads of the local church authorities. On the other hand, examples of tension between a Catholic party and the

Curia are known: the most remarkable was the refusal of the German Centre to vote for the *Septennat* (seven-year military law) although invited to do so by the Holy See in 1887. This episode marked a turning-point in the relations between the Centre and the Curia, leading to the development of a more 'German' and less 'Roman' orientation in Windthorst's party. This affair shows that Catholic parties were not the secular arm of the Holy See, but it confirms the fact that the study of Catholic parties cannot ignore Vatican policy and its repercussions.

For certain Christian Democrats the acceptance of political democracy meant the affirmation of political autonomy with regard to the Church, freedom from denominationalism, collaboration with unbelievers, liberals and even socialists, and the acceptance of laws which no longer gave the Church a privileged status. From that point onwards, internal tensions were acute. The 'Christian democrats' who opposed the proponents of a denominational and 'integralist' line were reviving the tradition of a liberal Catholicism which had been condemned by the Syllabus of Pius IX and which they themselves, at the beginning, had appeared to reject. Many conflicts, condemned by the hierarchy, provide examples of these divisions.

Throughout the history of Catholic parties, similar sequences of events have been seen to take place: first, men proclaim their desire to base themselves on a Catholic foundation, to express the demands of Christianity in face of the social structure and civil society. Then appears the dream of a Christian State and political system, which is inseparable from a certain degree of rejection of the present world and the hope of its transformation under the influence of Christianity. In this respect the Catholic parties are involved with a millenarian vision of social regeneration. Then the time of rejection and hope is succeeded by the harsh revelation of the constraints of politics, which belongs to a different order from that of religion. For some, this is the stage of non-denominationalism and the discovery of the values which are proper to the profane order. For others, it is a time of transition from mysticism to politics and the realities of power and government. Thus, Catholic parties lived between two poles, one religious, the other political. This tension was the source of the originality of their history and, perhaps more generally, of the history of those movements, Christian in inspiration, which are engaged in the world. Between the affirmation of the necessity of a political system inspired by Christianity and that of the autonomy of politics, how many have been the partial compromises and the complicated wanderings.

Of course, the evolution of the Church, and of the issues at stake in political struggles, has tended towards the withering away of the properly denominational aspects of Christian Democratic parties, which have thus lost the ambiguous status they once had. They are becoming genuinely, and not just ideally, non-denominational parties. But they preserve, whether or not they call themselves Christian, a relationship, if not to the social and political teaching of Christianity—'the Bible is not a book of blueprints' declares the programme of the CDU—at least to the world-vision which Christianity proclaims. In this, they are different from pragmatic parties for managing the system, on the American model. The remain *Weltanschauungsparteien* within which different tendencies exist, some conservative, some democratic or even socialistic. This very diversity is a sign of vitality and at least counsels the historian to remain prudent when predicting the future of this type of political organisation.

Translated by L. H. Ginn

PART II

The Political Role the Church Actually Plays

Helmut Geller

Class Membership and Church

WHEN WE talk about the class structure of a society, we are talking about inequality in this society, inequality in education, in income, in jobs, in influence, in attitudes and in social images. Here we are presupposing that the criteria for measuring inequality have a decisive influence on the individual's experienced world and hence on the way he thinks and experiences the world.

Researchers have demonstrated influences of this kind on different variables. Thus for example Kreutz[1] shows the connection between parents' income and children's reward and the latter's level of ambition. The level of ambition is determined by the level of reward and desire-satisfaction in the past. The higher the reward in the past for the same effort, the higher will be the expected reward. On the other hand as reward increases a more ideal standard of living is felt to be attainable, resulting in more energy being expended to achieve it. But if the ambitions, expectations and goals are fixed at a relatively high level, they are also very vulnerable, because those concerned are in an exposed position. This causes such people to incline towards a relatively marked caution and scepticism *vis-à-vis* others. They live at a considerable 'distance' from others. Since the level of reward depends on income, it is clear how income also influences the way people think.

One's position at work also has an influence on one's way of thought. Bahrdt and others[2] show that, in many firms where workers are presented with unworkable regulations, they evolve their own norms. Taken together with the experience of having no influence this often leads to a 'them-and-us' dichotomy in their view of the world. They experience the world predominantly as 'opposition'. Moore and Kleining's[3] characterisation of the individual strata, too, demonstrates the connection between job and behaviour and ways of thought.

Social inequality arises, therefore, because the members of a society live in different contexts of experience. As a result of these different contexts they form different ways of thinking, feeling and reacting. These different ways of thinking, feeling and reacting create barriers to interaction, making it difficult for people living in these different contexts to understand one another. Pappi proposes the following criterion for differentiating class strata: 'We speak of social strata only when prestige differences between occupations affect behaviour in such a way that prestige equality leads to more frequent primary contacts on the part of those in the jobs concerned, and that we can observe interruptions in the frequency of interaction at particular points in the prestige continuum.'[4] He operationalises primary contacts in regard to the choice of friends. The choice of spouse would yield even greater differentiation.

If one describes the social structure in terms of contexts of experience which lead to knowledge-systems with respectively typical ways of thinking, feeling and reacting, in such a way that interaction with fellow members of society who do not share these contexts is made difficult, it is clearly inadequate, in distinguishing class, to describe the social structure merely in terms of income and job. Other factors must be adduced such as generation, sex, language group and nationality. These contribute to the individual's knowledge-system and lead to statistically measurable limitations on interaction at the borders of these experience contexts. Thus religion is also a factor in social class. For belonging to a particular religious group influences the individual's ways of thinking, feeling and reacting. The barriers to interaction between members of different religious groups are also clearly measurable.

Even today there is still a relevant difference between the Catholic and Protestant modes of thought in the ethical evaluation of actions. As a result of training for confession, Catholics are inclined to see moral norms as a system of rules laid upon them by Church authorities. Faith is understood more as a recognition of an authority which makes demands and can punish. Subjectivity is expressed predominantly only in the degree to which the norms are kept. Yet a merely minimal satisfying of these demands produces guilt. In a certain sense faith becomes de-subjectivised. Observing norms is evaluated independently of inner attitude. Personal reservations have no effect on the content of the demands. The relation of actions to these norms is treated casuistically.

Protestants judge their behaviour otherwise. For them the individual act is less relevant to salvation than the attitude of mind. The only important thing is to intend the good and strive for it. Therefore one must develop one's personality. Schmidtchen writes: 'The German Protestant cannot base his justification on works but only on an inner process: on a good conscience, on the awareness of divine power; good actions follow automatically from this.'[5] We can see from mixed marriages, in the couple's life together, how these different ways of thought influence behaviour. Even after a long period of life together, the one partner seldom understands the other partner's ethical evaluation of actions.

A society's stratification is not one-dimensional. In any one society there are different class hierarchies or class systems.[6] A class system can be defined as a hierarchy of classes based on a single criterion. Every class system in a society embraces all the members of this society. Thus every member of German society belongs simultaneously to one of the classes whose criteria are job, wealth, education, age, sex, religious affiliation and residence. Each class system results in a particular knowledge-system.

Knowledge-systems of classes in the various dimensions are compatible or incompatible in different degrees. Hence some combinations are more possible than others. The more compatible two such systems are, the less cognitive discord will be experienced by someone who belongs to both. This is one reason why religious affiliation is closely correlated with particular class membership in other dimensions. In what follows we shall indicate these correlations in the case of the German Catholic population. Such correlations cannot be regarded as chance, on the one hand if they are more markedly exhibited by Church leaders, and on the other hand if the classes concerned participate more in Church activities than other classes of the same class system.

In 1970 44·6 per cent of the population of the Federal Republic were Catholics. Their residence (distribution between town and country) differs sharply from that of the other religious groups. In communities of less than 500 inhabitants Catholics are under-represented, in communities of 500-1,000 inhabitants their percentage matches that of the total population, and in communities of 5,000-10,000 inhabitants 52 per cent are Catholics. From then on the proportion of Catholics in the population diminishes as the community size increases. In middle-sized towns the percentage is 38·6 per cent and in large cities 36·8 per cent. A parallel tendency is evident in participation in Church life: in small communities the proportion of church attendance among Catholics is high, decreasing with the size of the population centre. Furthermore, a disproportionate number of priests come from country parishes. In 1971 44 per cent of priests in the Federal Republic were recruited from villages and country parishes, and a further 19 per cent from small towns. So as the location increases in size there is a drop in the Catholic proportion of the total population, in church attendance among Catholics, and in the quota of men who feel called to the priesthood. The more a community is marked by liberal attitudes and industrialisation, the more cognitive discord is felt *vis-à-vis* the Catholic way of thought.

Max Weber[7] demonstrated the differences between Catholic and Protestant thought in relation to industrial, capitalist thought. Now the latter mode of thought is the dominant one in the Federal Republic, and the education system (which substantially determines one's chances of professional success) is geared to it. This results in Catholics having less educational motivation than Protestants or those of no religious affiliation.[8] Since 1900 Germany has exhibited a Catholic educational deficit. These are the figures for school leavers in religious groupings: in 1970, for every 100 of the adult population of each group over 25 years of age, who had completed school education, 25 of the unaffiliated had a higher qualification than the school-leaving certificate; for Protestants the number was 24; for Catholics it was 19. Related to the total population the Catholic deficit was as follows: those who completed technical school: 18 per cent; matriculation: 25 per cent; engineering college: 23 per cent; university: 12 per cent. Although this deficit had shrunk in the case of those still in the education system, it was still not in proportion. The choice of job also demonstrates that this is attributable to the Catholic mentality. Catholics prefer careers in social and teaching areas, whereas Protestants and especially the unaffiliated prefer science, technology and economics.

One consequence of low educational qualifications is the lower proportion of Catholics in prominent social positions. They are under-represented among the self-employed in big business, in the professions, among higher civil servants and upper and middle executives. Even among leaders of the work force they are proportionally under-represented.

This is matched by the income structure of Catholics, which compares unfavourably with that of the other religious groups. They are particularly strongly represented in the lower income bracket, under-represented in the middle income bracket, and at the top they are far below their proportion.

Nellesen-Schumacher[9] relates this situation to a tension Catholics experience with regard to the technical and scientific area. The deficit is particularly apparent in the case of chemists, physicists, mathematicians and biologists. Catholics are also poorly represented in finance. The more a profession depends on a scientific or capitalist approach, the less participation there will be by Catholics. Here, too, we see that the Catholic way of thought is less compatible than the Protestant with the scientific and capitalist way.

A look at the social background of priests would suggest the same conclusion. The priests in the Federal Republic are, to a disproportionate degree, frequently the sons of farmers. Roughly corresponding to the population average, the priests' fathers were members of the professions, proprietors of larger businesses or employees. But measured against the total population workers are under-represented among the priests' fathers. Here, however, we come up against the problem of relating the figures, for in the Federal Republic the priesthood is an academic profession; and the background of academics is substantially different from that of the total population. Comparing the background of candidates for the priesthood in 1974 with that of the total of third-level students in 1971, one gets a different picture. Whereas 13 per cent of candidates for the priesthood gave 'farmer' as their father's occupation,[10] the figure for all students in scientific faculties was only 4 per cent; 26 per cent of the candidates' fathers were workers whereas only 12 per cent of all students' fathers were; 11 per cent of the candidates came from families of tradesmen as against only 4 per cent of all students. There was a relatively equal representation of sons of senior employees among candidates for the priesthood and other students. On the other hand the proportion of sons of ordinary employees (13 per cent; 24 per cent), higher civil servants (11 per cent; 14 per cent), middle and lower civil servants (8 per cent; 13 per cent), and professional men (4 per cent; 8 per cent) was substantially higher for all students than for candidates for the priesthood. Analogously to the decrease in the percentage of Catholics in an occupation group, there is a drop in candidates for the priesthood whose fathers are in these occupations. The decline in vocations to the priesthood is in part attributable to the shrinkage of those occupation classes from which until recently the majority of priests were recruited.

An affinity can be observed between the Catholic knowledge-system and conservative classes, which are influenced only slightly in their mode of thought by industrialist-capitalist thought. To the extent that, as a result of social change in the Federal Republic, these classes lose members, there is a drop in participation in church attendance and ministrations. This process is reinforced by the fact that Catholics in the Federal Republic are politically emancipated; now, by contrast to the nineteenth century, they can exert influence on the political system. Political equality of rights for the religious groups meant that it was no longer necessary, for self-preservation, to draw a clear boundary between oneself and others, with the result that people became more aware of common ground shared with other religious groups. Next the religious boundaries lost a lot of their importance for everyday activity, so that outside influences could make themselves felt more in the Catholic area.

In order to understand the effects of class ties on conservative, pre-industrial, capitalist classes, we must mention a few more theoretical considerations. We have seen that the individual member of several classes is in different class-systems at the same time. Each of these classes produces a particular way of thinking, feeling and behaving. We must not imagine, however, that these knowledge-systems can be deduced from class membership. The attitude inherent in a class can be couched in other modes of thought, can be modified or suppressed by them. The mode of thought most strongly influencing the individual depends on the relevance he attributes to membership of his class. He will determine the boundaries of the roles he plays according to the class membership to which he attaches priority and the interpretation which he regards as best defining his situation. He will adopt its views of the boundaries between the various areas and incorporate the other class memberships as roles in his knowledge-system, thus limiting their competence to clearly-defined fields. He permits the dominant class to limit the autonomy of the other classes.

However, the influencing of knowledge-systems of classes both above and below is not a unilateral operation. Even the interests of a lower class enter into the knowledge-system of the dominant class. But since the individual experiences his whole knowledge-system as a unity, it is often hard for him to decide which knowledge elements can be attributed to which class.

If, in recruiting for positions of leadership, the Church takes membership of pre-industrial classes as a principle of personnel selection, the influence of these classes in the Church and the Church's decisions will be particularly strong. To the extent that an influence of this kind on Church decisions runs counter to the complex of interests of other classes, members of such classes will have a low evaluation of the relevance of Church decisions, and will distance themselves from the Church as an institution.

Translated by Graham Harrison

Notes

1. See H. Kreutz 'Die zeitliche Dimension von Sozialisationsumwelten. Schulbildung, Zukunftsbezug, Selbsteinschätzung und soziale Anpassung von Jugendlichen aus verschiedenen sozialen Schichten' in *Sozialisationsforschung* ed. H. Walter (Stuttgart 1975) III pp. 107-150.

2. See H. P. Bahrdt et al. *Das Gesellschaftsbild des Arbeiters. Soziologische Untersuchung in der Hüttenindustrie* (Tübingen 1957).

3. H. Moore and G. Kleining 'Das soziale Selbstbild der Gesellschaftsschichten in Deutschland' in *Kölner Zeitschrift für Soziologie und Sozialpsychologie* 12 (1960) 86-119.

4. F. U. Pappi 'Sozialstruktur und soziale Schichtung' in *Kölner Zeitschrift für Soziologie und Sozialpsychologie* 25 (1973) 23-74, n. 25.

5. G. Schmidtchen *Protestanten und Katholiken* (Berne 1973) p. 149.

6. G. Lenski *Power and Privilege. A Theory of Social Stratification* (New York 1966).

7. M. Weber *Die protestantische Ethik und der Geist des Kapitalismus*, and *Gesammelte Aufsätze zur Religionssoziologie* 1 (Tübingen ⁶1972).

8. Details in T. Nellesen-Schumacher *Sozialprofil der deutschen Katholiken. Eine konfessionsstatistische Analyse* (Mainz 1978).

9. *ibid*, p. 135.

10. Details in G. Schmidtchen *Umfrage unter Priesteramtskandidaten* (Freiburg 1975) p. 8.

Guy van den Brande

The Political Role of Papal Diplomacy

FEW WOULD deny that today the Catholic Church plays an important and wide-ranging part in international politics. There are the statements made by Popes Paul VI and John Paul II in the General Assembly of the United Nations and by their representatives in its specialised institutions, all clearly aimed at the world-wide community. Then there are the official positions taken up by papal delegates at international conferences. Moreover, the Holy See has permanent diplomatic relations with some eighty States which show no political or religious unity. The recent widespread journeys of John Paul II have stirred up not only the country actually visited but roused the attention of Catholics and non-Catholics throughout the world.

But these are only a few illustrations of the international presence of the Church.

Before, however, analysing in more detail the various ways in which the Holy See intervenes, it might be useful to clarify the international juridical position of the Church in general and in the family of the United Nations in particular.[1]

1. THE JURIDICAL BASIS OF THE CATHOLIC CHURCH IN INTERNATIONAL LAW[2]

Because of the fluid international context of the Catholic Church there is both terminological and epistemological confusion between three distinct entities: the Catholic Church as such, Vatican City and the Holy See.

On 11 February 1929, the representatives of the Holy See and the Italian Government signed the Lateran Treaty. This put and end to the so-called Roman question. The Treaty again recognised the Holy See's full sovereignty over a definite territory, although this was reduced to a minimum. The preamble to the Treaty clearly shows that the Holy See needs a visible token to enable it to fulfil its mission also at international level with complete independence. This was why it was deemed necessary to grant the Holy See full sovereignty over Vatican City. It is a kind of State but used as a means, namely, to provide a territorial guarantee for a spiritual independence. From a realistic point of view the 'State' is rather hard to discover.[3]

Apart from a few exceptions[4] the Holy See constantly operates in the world at large as head of the Catholic Church. It is in this function that it enjoys this international recognition.

34

That this Vatican City was a purely juridical and technical device is evident from the fact that recognition of the international status of the Holy See persisted when, on the one hand, the Papal States had disappeared and, on the other, Vatican City did not yet exist. This lasting international recognition in the absence of any secular authority shows that even in those days, and still more today, this recognition was based on the spiritual sovereignty of Church. This spiritual sovereignty in turn was based on deep-rooted juridical and social arguments in a centuries-old practical reality. It is analogous to, but not identical with, that of a State. It is rooted in a grouping which is distinct (based on purely spiritual values), organised (there is a definite hierarchy), and goes its own independent way, freely taking such measures as it deems opportune for its mission or its unity.

Strictly speaking, the term 'Holy See' refers to the function of the pope whose authority flows from a double sovereignty: as head of the Catholic Church and as secular leader of the State of Vatican City. In the broader sense it covers the whole complex of congregations, tribunals, offices and commissions which are responsible for the government under the authority of the pope. One must clearly differentiate between the 'Catholic Church' and the 'Holy See': they are two distinct entities. The Catholic Church is the whole group of people who have gathered round Jesus Christ; the Holy See is only the highest hierarchical authority of this Church and of Vatican City.

2. THE INTERNATIONAL PRESENCE OF VATICAN DIPLOMACY AND ITS POLITICAL ROLE

It is necessary to keep in mind the dual function of papal representation: its task is both internal and external.

According to the *Motu Proprio Sollicitudo Omnium Ecclesiarum* of 24 June 1969 the most important task of papal representatives is to ensure the contact between the central authority of the Church and the local churches. This should not be taken to mean that it is only a way in which central authority can control the local churches. The point is rather that the ideas and movements which develop in the local churches are adequately fed back into the central authority. So one might describe the first task of a papal representative as ensuring closer contact between the local churches and the Holy See and to make this contact more effective.

The second function of the papal representative (and this is often the case) is to represent the Holy See at local or national government level or in an international organisation. At this level he is subject to the rules of international law and acts as a genuine papal ambassador. The development of this classical bilateral diplomacy has led the Holy See to attach constantly more serious attention to various international institutions, and in various ways.[5] In this area it seems particularly to concentrate on two major groupings: the United Nations and the inter-governmental institutions of Europe.

The Church's interest in the international institutions and particularly in the United Nations dates from their very beginnings. It must be admitted that the Church will only play the part of the back-seat driver. In successive statements it left no doubt about its sympathy with a world-organisation whose sole purpose was to pursue the peace which the Church is so concerned about. The UN is a means to press forward towards this peace and this needs to be encouraged: 'Today the bonds of mutual dependence become increasingly close between all citizens and all the peoples of the world. The universal common good needs to be intelligently pursued and more effectively achieved. Hence it is now necessary for the family of nations to create for themselves an order which corresponds to modern obligations, particularly with reference to those numerous regions still labouring under intolerable need. . . . The international agencies, both universal and regional, which already exist, assuredly deserve well of the human race. These stand forth as the first attempts to lay international foundations under the whole human community for the solving of the critical problems of our age, the promotion of global progress, and the prevention of any kind of war.'[6]

In his address to the UN on 4 October 1965, Paul VI compared what the UN did on the secular level with what the Catholic Church would like to achieve on the spiritual level. Fourteen years later John Paul II pointed once again to the vital historical value of the UN as the one and only truly international forum.[7] These are but a few instances of the way in which the Holy See has repeatedly shown the importance it attaches to support for the UN.

But the Holy See also takes a more active part in what the UN is doing. It is a member of an impressive amount of specialised agencies, among which the United Nations Conference on Trade and Development (UNCTAD), the United Nations Industrial Development Organisation (UNIDO), the High Commission for Refugees (UNHCR) and the International Atomic Energy Agency (IAEA) are some of the most important. It has a permanent representative at UN Headquarters in New York, and in the UN Geneva Office, in the World Health Organisation (WHO), its International Labour Organisation (ILO), the UN Educational, Scientific and Cultural Organisation (UNESCO), the United Nations Children's Fund (UNICEF), on the Economic and Social Council (ECOSOC).

Here, too, there is an anomaly where Vatican City is concerned. Because of its territorial independence the Holy See joined the United Nations on this basis too as a member of some specific organisations from the very beginning. It would never have dreamt of its present position without this advantage, even though its interventions are practically always inspired by its spiritual dimension. No other religion or religious organisation enjoys this kind of status. Yet, this was made possible because of its position.

In its interventions at the UN the Holy See has always respected the territorial sovereignty of other States and kept well aloof from issues that were politically loaded. Nor has it ever tried to use the UN as a pulpit in favour of ecclesiastical or religious advantages. The usual practice has been to back universally valid principles. This area is pre-eminently the concern of the UN and on the whole this is in harmony with the Christian message.

In such international institutions the representatives of the Holy See have the advantage of wearing no political label. They can even do their job with more flexibility than the ordinary nuncio who has been delegated by a particular government. The nuncio is constantly preoccupied with the balance between ecclesiastical authority and the local community on the one hand, and between both these and the government on the other. In an international institution there is a more open-ended atmosphere which allows each member to act freely. The very purpose of such international institutions is more favourable to this freedom than the twofold bilateral relationships the traditional ecclesiastical diplomat can afford.

The fundamentally neutralist attitude of the Holy See towards politics and economics has so far made it shy away from full membership of the UN. Moreover, article 4 of the UN's charter explicitly mentions 'States'. The Catholic Church is not a State, unless once again one wants to get around this point by referring to the status of Vatican City.

Without delving into the basic principles which determine the international stance of the Holy See,[8] the question arises what real influence the Holy See can exert at the international level since it has no realistic economic, political or military backing. It clearly has at its disposal a fair amount of approaches which amount to more than the assertion of symbolical and/or historical prerogatives. As an international personality the pope has a certain amount of power and influence which derive from his function and the way the Catholic Church works as a whole.[9]

Power does not simply consist in the matter of armed forces but also in the power of persuasion. The power of persuasion is linked with the prestige of the persuader. It is clear that the pope and his representatives as an emanation of the Catholic Church may claim some considerable integrity in humanitarian socio-cultural matters. Their commitment to such matters is of a different kind from that of the normal international participants and surveys these issues from another point of view. The personality and charisma of the pope can strengthen the right approach.

The fact that the pope heads a 'world-organisation' such as the Catholic Church with a highly centralised government allows the pope to be better informed about what is happening in any part of the world. The sorting out of all this information, not only at the religious level but also at that of cultural, social and political interest, may make papal diplomacy one of the best informed, if not 'the' best in the world. Moreover, it so happens that in some countries only the Church still has some political elbow-room. Its world-wide presence through humanitarian organisations also provides this papal diplomacy with many valuable details which strengthen its function.

The present exceptional international and juridical framework of papal diplomacy creates unlimited possibilities for this papal diplomacy to exploit for its world-wide mission.

3. PAPAL DIPLOMACY AT THE DISARMAMENT CONFERENCE OF THE UN

Since 1964 the Holy See has had a permanent observer at New York. In this way the Holy See plays its part in the annual General Assembly of the UN. Of the six large commissions set up in the General Assembly which meet annually, the first deals with security and disarmament.

In the course of the activities of this first commission as they are brought up in the General Assembly the first intervention of the Holy See took place in 1974 in the 29th General Assembly, and since then regularly almost every year. On the whole there is only one such intervention in the 50 to 60 working sessions per general session. The reason for this may be that the Holy See only takes part as an accredited observer, on the one hand, and that it wishes to maintain its political neutrality on the other. We find therefore no concrete proposals or specific interventions with relation to clearly defined subjects. It rather aims at stressing the moral and humanitarian aspect where matters of principle are concerned.

What is the Holy See mainly concerned with when it intervenes in this Disarmament Commission?

Not bound by any political allegiance, the Holy See stresses that its sees disarmament as essentially a moral problem and which, as a spiritual authority, it naturally is concerned with.

The starting-point is its postulate that true peace can be achieved only through disarmament. Peace through armament is no real peace. The arms race has to be condemned without reservation, not only because of the inherent violence of its nature and the eventual direct consequences of its use but just as much because of its fundamental injustice with regard to mankind. Armament is a human theft because it takes away the very means of production so desperately necessary to provide a large part of the world-population with a more human condition of life. Technical progress is being used to make more sophisticated weapons instead of improving the lot of mankind. There is in fact a close connection between armament and development.

In order to bring about this disarmament it is imperative that the structures of economic production be turned from means leading to death and destruction into means serving the cause of life.

As a second and frequently repeated condition the Holy See stresses the necessity of an international control which must be strict and effective. This requires a society which is internationally organised and, while safeguarding the sovereign rights of every State, can effectively supervise the general well-being of all.[10] The Holy See recognises that the problem of disarmament is far from simple because of its complex and technical nature. On this issue a maximal consensus should be reached at world-level, and it should be clear that disarmament is closely tied up with the whole spectrum of fundamental human rights.

4. THE EUROPEAN CONFERENCE ON DISARMAMENT AND CO-OPERATION

The Holy See took part from the beginning in the preparations for this Conference, and later on in the Conference itself. This Conference later led to the so-called Helsinki Agreement. The Conference continued its work in other European cities, such as Belgrade and, most recently, Madrid. In contrast with the European countries the attitude of the Holy See stands out for its universalist approach. It indeed represents not merely a European but a world-wide Church. Compared with the positions taken up in the UN we see here only the occasional shift of emphasis. Peace cannot be built on the adage '*Si vis pacem, para bellum*' (If you want peace, prepare for war). The kind of peace which rests on equality of armament only creates a precarious balance which may be upset at any moment and implies the risk of an indefinitely on-going arms race. If we want peace, we should not prepare for war but build up peace.

Among the necessary conditions for such a peace the most important is justice. An unjust situation between various peoples and States makes a true peace impossible. This justice inevitably implies respect for every man's fundamental rights.

In the context of this European Conference the Holy See particularly stresses freedom of religion. Mgr Silvestrini's intervention in Belgrade on 7 October 1977, was almost wholly devoted to this freedom of religion.

The ultimate aim of peace and co-operation can be achieved only by common agreement and active co-operation.

All this leads one to conclude that the Catholic Church with its international presence and its papal diplomatic representatives may claim a broad international juridical basis to pursue its aims at that level. Generally speaking, the Holy See enjoys in this function more independence and prestige than the other actors in the field of international politics.

The framework exists, the matter is always relevant. So we may perhaps suggest that a more active and outspoken approach might be more profitable for the Church in particular and for mankind in general.

Translated by T. L. Westow

Notes

1. For recent and general treatment of this subject, see H. F. Köck *Die Völkerrechtliche Stellung des Heiligen Stuhls* (Berlin 1975, 913 pp.); Mgr H. E. Cardinale *The Holy See and the International Order* (Gerrards Cross 1976, 557 pp.).

2. H. Wagnon 'La Personnalité du Saint-Siège en droit international' in *Studia Diplomatica* 1977, 321-342.

3. The 'but étatique' as it is put by P. Ciprotti in 'The Holy See: Its Function, Form and Status in International Law' in *Concilium* 58 (1970) 63.

4. Thus the Holy See acts as head of the secular State of Vatican City in straightforward technical matters such as the Universal Postal Union (UPU) or the International Telecommunication Union (ITU).

5. For this, see N. Nucitelli *Le Fondement juridique des rapports entre le Saint-Siège et les Nations Unies* (Paris 1966), and F. Russo, SJ 'Le Saint-Siège at les organisations internationales' in *Etudes* (July 1976) 15-31.

6. *Gaudium et spes*, no. 84 (trs. W. M. Abbott *The Documents of Vatican II*, London 1966).

7. On the papal addresses, see Ph. Laurent 'L'Eglise et l'ONU à travers les discours de Paul VI et Jean-Paul II' in *Politique Etrangère* (March 1980) 115-127.

8. See H. de Riedmatten, OP 'Le Catholicisme et le développement du droit international' in *Recueil des Cours* 1976, III, 115-159.

9. J. D. Murphy 'The Papacy and the Secretary-Generalship: a study of the role of the exceptionally-situated individual actors in the international system' in *Co-existence* (July 1970) 165-181.

10. See also: M. Tricaud 'L'Encyclique *Pacem in Terris* et la création d'une autorité internationale' in *Rev. gén du droit international public* (1966) 117-128.

D

Piero Bellini

The Concordat Countries of Southern Europe

OF THE three Concordat countries of southern Europe (Italy, Spain and Portugal), the most interesting from the point of view of this subject is undoubtedly Italy. Its experiences (particularly more recent ones) can teach several lessons—of general application—on how central ecclesiastical bodies show their intentions with regard to Church participation in the affairs of the body politic, and on what further attitudes can reasonably be expected.

I am not here going into the consideration that it has been in Italy that (first on the lines of Germanic juridical culture and then in its own right) the system of ecclesiastical law has reached a particularly high degree of conceptual development. Nor do I propose to give too much weight to the fact that—alone among the concordats of southern Europe—the Italian one of 1929 is the only one to contain specific restrictive clauses designed to prevent the Church—in the form of either its ordained ministers or lay organisations—from lending its support to 'any political party'. (Precepts backed up by a series of repressive measures directed at bringing penal sanctions to bear on any priests found guilty of exciting contempt for civil laws or institutions, or of interfering in civil elections.)

What is more to the point is that Italy in the last fifty years has produced a series of occasions when it has been particularly vital for the Church to make its voice heard in the heart of the *civitas*. And the Church has intervened with some force: making its own 'political presence' felt in explicit and direct terms, without the slightest hesitation, and with greater authoritarian resolution than usual in earlier times. I am speaking of the furious controversies unleashed on the occasions of the introduction of divorce and the legalisation of abortion, in 1970 and 1978 respectively, which occupied the whole of Italian public opinion for years, both in the period when the laws were being framed and in the subsequent period when they were put to a *referendum* whose results were to be binding.

Both these cases were of such moral significance (besides their civic significance) that they pushed the ecclesiastical hierarchy into a more forceful mode of operating, driving them beyond the veiled and oblique style of intervention common in the past, into open, frontal attack. The hierarchy judged this approach to be so incumbent on them (as so intimately responding to the mission of the Church as Church) as to override any legal limitations. So (in the case of abortion) the main thrust of this reinvigorated interventionism was taken on, in the first place, by the pope himself, in his role as bishop of Rome and primate of Italy, and in that as head of the universal Church.

So these two episodes—even though both tied to some degree to the particularities of the political and ecclesiastical situation in Italy—are both really important enough to transcend the 'case of Italy' and take on general significance. They are also both indispensable parts of recent experience against which—once the passions of the moment have cooled—to judge the 'validity' of the Concordat system in itself.

It is a fact that the Concordat style of regime as such—simply because it is designed to establish a system of co-ordination between Church and State—starts from the principle of a sharing-out of operative spheres of respective ownership. This demarcation of the two provinces (ecclesiastical and civil) is based on 'types of matters', following guidelines provided by the traditional distinction between 'spiritual matters' and 'temporal matters'. So it postulates that all those 'affairs in real life' (the whole of that *res*) that relate to essentially religious values belong 'to the exclusive competence of the Church', while other affairs (those other 'social activities', made up of the various aspects of personal behaviour that go to make up human life) are left to the 'exclusive competence of the State', as relating purely to secular interests.

(So much so that—by virtue of this division—there is nothing left to their 'concurrent competence' except a restricted class of 'matters' (*res* here known as '*mixtae*') made up of just those concerns that display such an interweaving of the sacred and the profane that the only way to deal with them appears to be through bilateral juridical organisation.)

In this framework, the management of 'politics', understood in its wider sense, is naturally reserved to the exclusive authority of the State—'*reddite Caesari quae Caesaris*. Because—even if Concordats do not contain an explicit sanction of the authority of the State—this is 'presupposed' to belong to it. Which means to say that the usual guarantee of the '*libertas Ecclesiae*', taken as meaning that it has full power in all spiritual matters, can only be parallelled by a corresponding affirmation of the '*libertas Status*', of the sovereignty of the State in its own sphere.

Now, there is no denying the grave over-simplification to which this arrangement gives rise in practice, as can be seen to a fair degree in the ordinary workings of society. It should also be remarked that this solution is based on a false premiss. By relying on the notion that some 'matters' can belong 'to the exclusive interests of the State' and others 'to the exclusive interests of the Church', it clearly produces a sort of arbitrary 'vivisection' of human affairs as they are in reality. These are usually 'composite', essentially made up of diverse elements inextricably bound up with one another.

We must recognise (and the recent vicissitudes of Italian society are conclusive proof that we must) that in fact there are no real-life matters, no forms of 'human activity' to which the authoritative appreciation of both the Church and the State cannot be extended at one and the same time. A human action, even if it is a typical expression of religious life, cannot be entirely devoid of significance (unless it is 'merely permitted') for the State order. And an action that may be a typical expression of secular life, cannot fail to have its own (ethical and disciplinary) value in relation to Church order as well. What varies—in both types of judgment—is the 'parameter' which provides the standard for each of these acts in practice, a parameter formed in one case by the temporal values of State interests, and in the other by the spiritual values of Church interests. So what varies is the significance given to the same pieces of behaviour, which nevertheless, in themselves, remain exactly what they are.

(It must be said that the class of so-called 'mixed things'—*res mixtae*—far from embracing merely isolated cases in the totality of the twin jurisdictions, on the contrary represents an extremely broad category: to the point where it includes—at least potentially—virtually the whole of individual and collective behaviour.)

It goes without saying that—in the generality of cases—there will be a sufficient degree of compatibility in practice between the valuations made from both sides, so that they can operate in parallel without ever coming into conflict. There can of course be discord at times, but this need not be so acute that it cannot be resolved through an attitude of mutual tolerance. But it is a fact that—however the framework of relationships between Church and State has been put together, and whatever their goodwill towards one another—there will always be cases that cannot be resolved 'under the terms of the Concordat'. These cases arise when real-life problems come into play and produce a confrontation in which State and Church intervene as bearers of conflicting standards, which each feels (not necessarily unreasonably or wrongly) to be 'non-negotiable'.

The appraisal of the situation that one institution must carry out, if it is to be true to its own office, will then come into basic collision with the conflicting appraisal to which the other institution is in its turn committed, from analogous motives of fidelity to its own calling. It is precisely this inner cohesion of the two orders that leads inevitably to a 'formalisation of the conflict'.

I should say that the two recent episodes in Italian history adverted to have provided (both through the importance of the matter, and through the special circumstances surrounding it) just such occasions, and to an exceptional degree, in which—despite means of co-ordinating actions minutely detailed in the Concordat—this 'inevitability of conflict' was bound to show itself in a particularly acute form.

There were those in Italy (particularly during the referenda campaigns) who—in order to put a brake on the political interventions of the clergy—believed they could appeal to the Concordat, giving the restrictive ordinances of 1929, which were already in marked contrast to the libertarian principles of the Republican Constitution promulgated in 1948, an even more autocratic interpretation. And there were others who thought of appealing to the criminal code (however difficult this would be to reconcile with constitutional legitimacy) to punish priests who took advantage of their office to 'tie the hands of the electorate'. But, inevitably, the chief focus came to bear (in the case of the abortion debate) on the severe censures proclaimed by the pope. Here criticisms were not confined to challenging (a perfectly legitimate approach) the opportuneness of certain statements which seemed too inflexible; or to questioning the very correctness of the interpretation (which was at least debatable) put on the matter by the pope. Some went beyond this to deny—though it is difficult to see on what grounds—the very right of the bishop of Rome to pronounce authoritatively on such matters at all, as official authentic interpreter of Christian ethics or as chief custodian of ecclesiastical order.

Rather than discuss the merits of this juridical dispute, what seems more important is to draw from this event—so interwoven with civil and religious elements—a precept that will be generally valid, in view of foreseeable developments in the Church's mode of presence within the *civitas*. And I would say that recent events in Italy—with all the questions they have raised and all the reflections they have given rise to—should convince us of the need to move beyond the old bipartite view implicit in the Concordat system as such, which postulates the withdrawal of the political order from the magisterial, pastoral (and disciplinary) competence of the Church. These same events point rather to the need—both for the *ecclesia* and for the *civitas*—for a programme of 'liberalisation of their sectors'.

From the State, this would require full recognition (with no residual hesitation and no residual falling into regalistic-style temptations) of the legitimacy of the Church's ancient claim, ratified in the second Vatican Council, to '*spiritualiter de temporalibus judicare*': in the words of *Gaudium et spes*, 'She also has the right to pass moral judgments, even on matters touching the political order, whenever basic personal rights or the salvation of souls make such judgments necessary' (76g). It would then be up to the Church to impose a similar discipline on itself, in the wider interests of the *corpus christianorum*. It would be up to it to ensure that the political role of the clergy was confined—in harmony with the *apostolica actuositas* of the laity—to a level touching true 'evangelical counselling of the world', without falling (as can only too often happen) into harmful forms of husbanding the views of electors. This is essential if the good name of the *sancta Ecclesia Christi* is to be maintained.

Basically—viewing the question from the standpoint of a liberal, democratic State—what is at stake is a sort of 'appeal to integrity'. In effect, a system that calls itself liberal and democratic—and therefore dedicated to promoting the 'maximum of freedom for all'—cannot deny the Church the right to be the Church, nor the pope the right to be pope. It cannot fail to recognise their basic freedom to carry out their proper calling, which they claim applies to all mankind and to all social structures through which the human personality unfolds. Such a recognition involves integrity with respect to the pluralistic principles on which such a democratic State is based: it would be a basic contradiction of its own postulates to prevent one of the major thought systems present *in civitate* to make its presence felt in the forms that are most proper to it.

Of course there is no denying that those who claim to speak in the name of God thereby enjoy an advantage over those who do not presume to speak in any name other than their own. But such a privilege—clearly—will not be eliminated in practice by restrictive legislation, which is itself also bound to be largely ignored in practice, thanks to the weight of public opinion against its social illiberality, and the reluctance of the judiciary to enforce it. So this favourable position would only be reinforced—in the way things work out—by attempts on the part of the State to restrain the *libertas ecclesiae*.

Such discrimination against the Church (trying to reduce it to silence in certain circumstances) is inevitably destined—thanks to its overbearing nature which is plain to see—to be countered by a 'rejection reaction' on the part of a system that aspires to an organic liberal order. So—at the end of the day—an autocratic attitude on the part of the State cannot fail to produce a result contrary to what was intended in the first place.

In civil society (in those who form its political and intellectual currents), this must produce a frustrating, uncomfortable situation, partly because the '*recens civilitas*' lacks valid formulae to offer in place of those that moulded life in the past—still largely approved of—and partly because the lay world fears a confrontation which it does not think it can win. The situation for the Church is quite different: it sees new prospects opening up, thanks to the increased power of suggestion that—by a spontaneous psychological reaction—naturally accrues to its actions. It (the Church) in effect comes to enjoy a sort of 'interest phenomenon' (in the financial sense), by the fact of its prevailing—not necessarily by acquiring a martyr's halo, but through the sense of greater purpose and energy that generally goes with the act of deliberate infraction of a '*non licet*' that is widely held to be unjust. So the Church acquires a state of greater 'meritoriousness', which can in the end raise (by sublimating) the 'charismatic value' of its witness, and so give it the ecclesiastical benefit of greater 'credibility'.

Giving total freedom to the hierarchy to act as they think fit means in practice replacing the directive functions of the ecclesial authorities in their normal place (in a purely religious key), as the expression of an office that, by its very nature, requires to be exercised on people who have the real attributes of 'believers', people who believe in the Word made flesh and in the Church as continuation of his saving work, and who place their firmest hope of redemption in their membership of this mystical body of Christ. In accordance with their religious calling, believers—by viewing the Church in fixed terms which suit their own personal existence—are satisfying a real existential need, which they feel to be their inalienable right; they are—cut off from other forms of conditioning—obeying a purely fideistic impulse. (In which resides the real value of the witness that those faithful to Christ are bound to render through carrying out the tasks of the apostolate conferred on them by their calling.) This will be the Church—operating in a regime of total freedom—which is best able to pursue its mission of edification in the fullness of its dignity, without having to bow to external pressures, but also without having to show itself in the guise of obvious victim.

But—to conclude this point—there is no hiding the fact that a programme of 'radical liberalisation' such as that proposed here, can lead to other results corresponding to expectations of another sort. Indeed, if the question is seen in a broader perspective, taking account of later and secondary effects as well as immediate and direct ones, such a programme would obviously be capable—by a curious paradox—of moving the life of the *civitas* in the direction of a more advanced 'laicism'. This would be what happens if the fact of the presence of the Church in the civil order (of its 'political' presence, even) were 'normalised' to such an extent that it was brought back without any friction into the scheme of a proper 'critical and dialectical pluralism'.

The removal from the overt actions of the State of any residual forms of autocracy inspired by regalism (with a view simply to equalise conditions between believers and non-believers so that they can approach the ideological dispute from a position of parity) is a necessary step in the organic process of 'restructuring', and subsequently 'humanising', the role of the Church in civil society. Then the Church will no longer be seen as a singular, incomparable entity cut off from the world and above the world, enclosed in its own 'separateness', but as one of the great forces of ideas intervening (as it then should intervene) in the real historical process of the whole complex of the human community. It can then put forward its own specific societal project, opposed to others, while still remaining bound up—on a basis of parity—in a relationship of continual intellectual and practical competitiveness with the other political and cultural factors involved in furthering the human race.

It will then be able to carry out the dialectical processes of that 'critical ideological pluralism' (in which it will, thanks to continual intellectual stimulus, have regard to the needs of all citizens in their problems of living together) which strikes the basic note that distinguishes the 'laicity' of the modern liberal democratic State. Just as it will be the Church's task to question the adequacy of lay schemes, so it will be the lay thinker's task to defend his own postulates and go on to question the adequacy of religious schemes. And this confrontation should be able to produce a mutual enrichment. Furthermore— and on this note I must end—this renewed lay mode of viewing the presence of the Church in the civil order should not fail to produce its own dynamic repercussion, of a spiritual nature, in the field of the internal life of the *ecclesia* itself. Free critical and even polemical examination of the projects and actions of the Church—of its values and tasks and the processes it uses to put them into action—as part of the normal debate within the *civitas*, should serve to produce a franker examination of the ideas and sentiments that inspire religious experience, within the *communitas fidei*.

Translated by Paul Burns

Johannes Neumann

The Role of the Official Church in the German Federal Republic

THE TWO large churches, as 'high-level organisations, with powerful influence, and considerable organisational stability' (E. Weber), survived the collapse of the 'Third Reich' relatively unharmed. The democratic parties, and organisations like the trades unions which had been disbanded by the Nazis, had to begin by rebuilding their institutions and developing new programmes. Other organisations, such as the various boards and associations, had, like the public administration, been compromised by the conduct of their members or their representatives in the 'Third Reich'. All of them were obliged laboriously to begin again, under the guidance—often neither competent nor well-disposed—of the occupying powers.

The churches were spared this organisational reconstruction. Above all, the Catholic Church not only felt itself to be in some sense on the side of the victors but was treated and respected as such both by the Allies and by the population. In spite of all the facts of most recent history, it was regarded as the bastion of freedom. Thus the churches were able to secure for themselves a position of some importance in the reorganisation of the German States, and considerable influence on political affairs. The churches and their representatives, especially the bishops, were generally treated as having been persecuted by the Nazi regime, and no check was made on the behaviour of individuals. Those among the clergy who openly sympathised with National Socialism were treated as unfortunate exceptions and withdrawn from public duties. The favourable attitude towards National Socialism of many bishops, priests and leading laymen, who had seen it as the bulwark of the Christian and German way of life and as the champion in the struggle against those forces which were undermining German culture—bolshevism, socialism, and Jewish-inspired liberalism—was conveniently forgotten. The few 'courageous' statements made by bishops were presented as evidence of a fundamental, general and total opposition of the churches to the Nazi system, although they had been directed almost exclusively against the violation of convents, the infringement of concordats or the euthanasia of the (Christian) insane. In other words, the protests were concerned with the Church's own interests.

The concordats with the German States of Bavaria, Prussia and Baden have been deplored as unfortunate compromises, at the time they were made, by the Church leaders then in office. Yet after 1945 these, along with the concordat concluded with the National Socialist Central Government, were put forward as the inviolable legal basis of the relationship between State and Church.[1] The administrations which were being set up in the German States and municipalities took care not to infringe the—supposed— rights of the Church. This applied even to those administrations whose own position was far removed from that of the churches. They would not, and could not, allow themselves to be suspected of having continued the National Socialists' persecution of the churches. Added to this was the fact that the occupying powers saw in the German churches their most important allies, on whom they could rely for information on local people of influence, and who would be useful to them in caring for the population and (in the case of the Americans) in the denazification process.[2] It is remarkable how little serious attention is paid, in the statements of the German Catholic bishops after 1945, to the how and why of the catastrophe of National Socialism and the final defeat. If these questions are considered at all, it is only to bemoan the misfortune which all have to suffer because some people have behaved in a 'godless' way and have not obeyed the teachings of the Church.

However, the old themes very quickly re-establish themselves at the centre of episcopal statements: general immorality, threats to the virtue of chastity, the sanctity of the family, and Catholic denominational schools. The last of these is offered as the criterion by which Catholic voters are to test their elected representatives: 'We expect of representatives to whom Catholics give their vote, resolute support for the claims of the Church'.[3]

In connection with the drawing up of the Federal Constitution, the bishops stressed that Catholics wanted to ensure that the foundation stones for the construction of the nation should be 'anointed with reverence for God, and not laid in the shadows of irreligion. Every stone to be used should be fashioned and laid in accordance with God's plans, whether it be a question of inviolable personal rights, or of community responsibility, of the protection of the family and the sanctity of marriage, or of a child's right to life and the God-given right of parents to bring up their children in their own way, or whether it be the safeguarding of proprietary rights or the imposition of duties on property-owners. . . . The maintenance of the rights and freedom of the Church is of decisive importance for ensuring a Christian life-style in the nation. The voters, who by their votes appoint the builders, who in turn have the task of fashioning the nation, must be aware of this responsibility. . . . But those who have been elected by Christian people for the work of Christian construction have the sacred duty to act wholly according to the principles of Christ. . . .' With reference to the significance of the mass-media, the bishops continue: 'The way in which the script of a film is written, or the parts are played when it is shot, is not a matter of indifference.'[4] It is quite clear that in saying this they are not thinking of the artistic quality of what is produced. They were concerned not just to influence but to control every significant feature of society. However, the episcopal warning did not produce the desired political result. They set their goal too high, and were not able to reach it. Thus in their 'Pastoral message on the Constitution of the German Federal Republic' of 20 May 1949, the Federal German bishops regretted that the aim of 'giving every basic law a deeper religious meaning' had not been achieved. The question must remain open whether the bishops wished to calumniate the new Republic or to provoke it when they declared that the fact that the 'parliamentary body' had declined to speak of 'God-given' human rights must give rise to serious reflection. They particularly took exception to the fact that the right of parents to send their children to a religious State school had been violated. Therefore they declared solemnly in the name of the whole Catholic population: 'We can only see this basic law, which fails to give recognition to such an important and inalienable fundamental right (as that of parents), as a provisional measure.' They state explicitly that they cannot and will not relinquish these demands. Apparently the bishops could not imagine how they and the 'Catholic people' could maintain their unity without 'opponents' or survive without a 'struggle', for they give the warning: 'This rejection of our demands forces upon us a struggle which could have been avoided . . . if our solemn warnings had been heeded.' Evidently the bishops were unaware both of the arrogance of their attitude, and of the macabre nature of the wording they used: Hitler, too, always spoke of a 'struggle forced upon' him! Finally, with downright apocalyptic rhetoric, they call upon 'all our Catholic people' to 'defend the rights of parents, and freedom of conscience. Our people now know what important cultural questions . . . are calling for decision. In the coming election they will give the answer to the rejection of their lawful claims by the parliamentary majority in Bonn.' They conclude that 'in this fateful hour, bound together in love with all our German people', they feel and declare themselves ready to engage 'with all other forces of goodwill' in the task of 'healthy reconstruction'.[5]

The themes we have so far spoken of run like a red thread through all pastoral letters down to the present day. The explicit campaigning for members of parliament with a 'Christian viewpoint' fell off somewhat in the sixties. More effectively than through such verbal strong-arm acts, examples of which could easily be multiplied, the churches worked quietly and efficiently at the strengthening of their influence on public authority.

1. THE DEVELOPMENT OF INSTITUTIONAL SAFEGUARDS

The new German political system, dependent as it was on the occupying powers, largely lacked not only political authority but also, and especially, the necessary national self-consciousness and its symbols. The churches, invited or uninvited, stepped into this vacuum. They provided a framework for national festivals, for example the 'swearing in' of the office-holders of the new Republic, and made their own emblems available. They took part in devising and drawing up new social regulations and laws, whether through members of parliament who had joined parties which deliberately aimed to behave in a Christian way, or through exercising influence directly on political representatives themselves.

A year before the birth of the German Federal Republic, the Catholic Church set up a liaison office in Bonn to safeguard the interests of the Church in the national reconstruction. Out of this work-place of the German bishops in the seat of the Federal Government—the only one of its kind in the world—the so-called 'Catholic Bureau' was developed.[6] Today it controls working-parties and commissions on particular subjects, under the direction of experts in those fields, and it also maintains regular contacts with the secretariat of the German Bishops' Conference, the Central Committee of German Catholics, and the German Caritas association, as well as with Catholic Bureaux in the various federal States.

The Catholic Bureau represents the Catholic Church *officially* on matters as diverse as proposed legislation, the protection of the environment or of monuments, the promotion of films and the use of the mass-media, personnel problems in the army, and questions of finance. In addition, *personal* contact with the members of the Federal Parliament, with the (higher) officials of government ministries, and with personalities in public life, is maintained through the 'Wilhelm-Böhler-Club'. In this way the Church is not only informed in good time of any measures which may be planned at federal level, but is also able to take an active part in the preparatory work. Thus the Church is enabled to exert an influence in every field, and to play an appropriate part in government support for education, or development aid, or the care of foreigners.

Over the years, in agreement with the Holy See, Church bureaux have been established in the individual States of the Federal Republic. These are supported by the dioceses in the States, and chiefly serve to extend the influence of the Church at State level and in matters of State politics. The first bureau of this kind was set up in the fifties in Düsseldorf, under the title of 'Catholic Bureau of Nordrhein-Westfalen', and the last in 1974 in Stuttgart for the dioceses of Freiburg and Rottenburg. The 'Catholic Bureau' set up in 1965 in Lower Saxony and located in Hanover is the fruit of a concordat between the Holy See and the State of Lower Saxony, dated 28 February 1965. In Article 19 of the concordat, it was agreed that the contracting partners would maintain 'regular contact' in all 'matters concerning their relationship'. In Bavaria, relations between the State government and the Nunciature and episcopate are so close, and (practically) all areas of interest to the Church so well covered by the concordat, which has been frequently revised, that the Bavarian Church does not seem to have felt the need for a bureau. In the States, the main concerns of the bureaux are in the sector of educational and school-politics. However, they have to 'avoid dealing with those questions which fall within the jurisdiction of the Holy See or the Nunciature' (Foundation document of the Catholic Bureau in Saarbrücken). In this field they can serve only as informants. Here, as in the Catholic Church as a whole, therefore, there is the strictest hierarchical structure.

By means of these bureaux, the Catholic Church in the German Federal Republic has succeeded in creating a lobby which embraces all parts of the nation's life. In addition, the bureaux maintain contact not only with the political parties, but also with all socially relevant groups—with the trades unions, for example, and with institutions for promoting education and science. In the area of social life in particular, the Catholic Church has been able not only to introduce its concept of the 'subsidiarity principle' into the application of the law, but also to root it firmly in the general consciousness.

2. THE PARTICIPATION OF THE CHURCH IN PARTICULAR POLITICAL DECISIONS

It is not possible, within the framework of this short article, to demonstrate how, where, and in what ways the representatives of the Church have, by means of influence exerted on the discussions of State institutions and basic laws, already laid the foundations for its future stances. Rather, we shall simply indicate the areas in which Church interests may be promoted.

2.1 In the earliest years of the Federal Republic's existence, the concerted efforts of the German Church forced the legislature into the difficult situation of having to pass an unconstitutional law. What happened, briefly, was as follows: In Article 3, section 2 of the Constitution, it is clearly and firmly laid down that 'men and women have equal rights'. To avoid the danger that important declarations in the Constitution might be regarded—as with the Weimar Constitution—simply as 'guide-lines', the makers of the Constitution, in Article 117 §1, laid upon the legislature the obligation of ensuring that laws conflicting with this principle should be brought into conformity with the new Constitution by 31 March 1953 at the latest. However, the provisions relating to marriage and family law in the Civil Code, which had been in force since 1900, did in fact conflict with the new principle. The Church brought all its authority to bear in support of the right of the husband and father to make the final decision in all questions of marriage and family life. It was affirmed that the patriarchal, hierarchical structure of *every* marriage was based upon natural law and firm biblical and theological foundations.[7] In addition to making individual statements on the subject, the bishops sent letters to the Minister of Justice (on 12 January 1952) and to every member of the Federal Parliament (on 30 January 1953),[8] and also on 30 January 1953 issued a pastoral letter to all the faithful. The hierarchy engaged in a polemic against a 'false notion of equal rights', and objected that the draft prepared by the Ministry of Justice did not sufficiently take into account 'the facts of natural order'. They warned against a 'disregard of western, Christian legal and social traditions'. *Every* marriage and family was, 'in its essential structure, regulated by human *nature* and the *divine will*, in such a way that these could not be altered by the State'. The natural holder of the right to make the final decision was the husband and father (letter of 12 January 1952). In the letter of 30 January 1953 the German bishops set out their demands in detail, and called in effect for nothing less than a complete revision of the whole body of marriage and family law along the lines they suggested:

1. marriage law should take as its starting-point the fundamental indissolubility of marriage;
2. compulsory civil marriage should be abolished;
3. in accordance with the natural and divine ordering of things, the right to make the final decision must fall not only to the father but to the husband; and
4. a wife or mother should not be encouraged to work outside the home.

In their pastoral letter of 30 January 1953, the bishops declare the the husband is the head of his wife and children. Anyone who disputes this sets himself
—against God's word and the teaching of the Church,
—against the true nature of human love,
—against the authority of God, on which that of the husband is modelled.
The bishops maintain that these principles should apply in *every* marriage, including non-Christian ones. The pastoral letter warns of the imminence of apocalyptic decisions: 'Marriage and the family are at stake. The foundations of our people's future are at stake. The Kingdom of God is at stake!' Because of this strong resistance of the Catholic Church to the 'subversive proposals for a false reform', which ultimately 'had as their aim the nationalisation of the family',[9] it was not until 18 June 1957 that the law could be finally passed by the Bundestag. By a narrow majority, the 'right of the husband to make the final decision' ('casting vote') was inserted, with a proviso concerning its abuse. The Federal Constitutional Court has, however, declared this much-disputed provision (§§ 1628 and 1629 section 1 BGB) null and void, because it is incompatible with the Constitution.

2.2 The Works Committee Law, passed in 1920 in the Weimar Republic, prescribed works committees for all businesses with more than twenty employees. The law applied not only in private industry, but also to the public service. There was no special provision for the Church sector. The National Socialists suspended this law. After 1945, ecclesiastical lawyers put forward the thesis that service in the Church was a matter 'neither of work-law, nor of public-law, but of church-law'.[10]

The Government's draft of a new industrial constitution (1950) proposed that the new law should not apply to the public administration and the public law corporations, but included the Church and its charitable and educational organisations among the special services for which at some points there would have to be particular provisions. The churches saw this as threatening the autonomy guaranteed to them by Article 137 section 3 of the Weimar Constitution. The President of the Council of Evangelical Churches in Germany, Bishop Dibelius, and the President of the Fulda Bishops' Conference, Cardinal Frings, in close ecumenical co-operation, made representations in almost identical terms, on 12 June and 28 July 1951 respectively, to Chancellor Adenauer and the Minister of Labour. They demanded that the law should not apply to 'employees of religious bodies and their organisations . . . whatever their legal form'. Under pressure from the churches, the CDU/CSU group declared that service in church institutions was not comparable with that in industrial concerns, and that some exceptional provision would have to be made. Such exceptional provision was included by the Bundestag in the Industrial Constitution of 1952 (and 1972) (§ 118 section 2), and also in the federal law of 5 August 1955 (§ 96) concerning workers' representation. It was then left to the churches to make their own regulations for the representation of their employees. Thus more than half a million employees in church organisations, mainly in the fields of education and welfare, within the two main churches, are deprived, at a vital point, of the protection of 'the law which applies to everybody'.[11]

2.3 The Church in the Federal German Republic has contrived to establish for itself rights of participation and secure positions in almost every socially relevant institution. Neither of the two main churches has fallen behind the other in this respect. By virtue of legal guarantees, the representatives of the Church have a say in such matters as radio and television councils, film censorship, press councils, and welfare organisations. This legal basis was, for the most part, achieved as a result of the use of pressure by the churches, on a vast scale. Thus, in relation to the television and radio authorities, for example, the churches are represented not only in the respective 'councils', but also through their own television and radio commissioners, and to some extent through special 'church commissioners' for 'news broadcasts'.

2.4 Catholic ideology and Church interests are most clearly reflected in social legislation. German social law is governed by the so-called 'subsidiarity principle', according to which, while it is the task of the State to guarantee social rights, the implementation of them is the responsibility, in the first instance, of non-State associations, the so-called 'free' youth and welfare organisations (Federal Social Welfare Law of 1970/71, especially §§ 5 section 2, 14 section 1, 2.6 and the decision of the Constitutional Court of 18 July 1967). Similarly the attempt of the coalition parties and the Federal Government to reform the Youth Welfare Law at certain significant points is at present being frustrated by the resistance of the churches, which support the CDU/CSU Opposition. Again the churches fear the 'nationalisation of the family'. The following points are in dispute: the rights of parents, the right of young people to share in family decisions, the relationship of public officials to the 'free' Youth Welfare Associations.

2.5 Questions of self-determination and joint responsibility, of values and of the moral basis of our society, were at the heart of the long-drawn-out arguments about the Criminal Law Reform measure (1974) and the Marriage Law Reform measure (1977). Because of the changes which were proposed, and because the concept of 'the democratisation of all areas of life' impinged upon church concerns, the Church was deeply involved in discussion of the problems. In obvious accord with certain memoranda produced, on the basis of totally different presuppositions, by the German Evangelical Church, the Catholic Church made its position clear 'On the reform of the Civil Divorce Law' (1970), 'On social development in the Federal Republic' (1972), 'Against Violence and Terror' (1977) and on the 'Causes of terrorism and the conditions necessary for overcoming it' (1978), as also on the problem of 'Social values and human happiness' (1976). The views of the bishops were also supplemented by declarations of the Central Committee of German Catholics, for example on the question of democratisation and on the problem of values. Such statements have normally ended with the demand that the democratic State should acknowledge concepts of value which are generally recognised, which can be derived form natural law, and which are based on the commandment of God, that it should bring its own legal provisions into line with them, and that it should then act accordingly.[12]

3. THE CHURCH'S CLAIM TO SOLE POWER OF REPRESENTATION

In connection with the relationship of the Church with the modern State, we must take note of a most revealing development in the political dimension. Whereas at the beginning of the democratic parliamentary life of the German States in the nineteenth century, Church interests were represented primarily by the priests and laymen of so-called 'political Catholicism', the Holy See was later anxious to bring its influence to bear directly, as it were, from 'government to government'.

With a view to weakening the parliamentary political representation of 'political Catholicism', the National Socialists had taken pains to ensure that a so-called 'depoliticising clause' was included in the Reichskonkordat (based on the Italian concordat with Fascist Italy in 1929). At this point, therefore, the interests of the two parties to the agreement coincided—though on different grounds. Article 32 of the Reichskonkordat forbade priests and clergy to engage in party-political activity. The Church, and especially the Holy See, thought that, thanks to the concordats, they could ensure closer contacts through the Nunciature and the bishops, by dispensing with the participation of clergy in political affairs. In fact, of course, this simply brought about the position provided for in the Church's legal documents (c. 139 § 4 CIC). After 1945, Catholic priests only became politically involved in isolated cases, and then usually in 'Christian' parties. However, when at the end of the sixties more and more priests were raising their voices in support of other parties and even recruiting for them, the German bishops prohibited priests from taking part in public party-political activities (27 September 1973).[13] The question whether the bishops were entitled to act in this way, since such matters are the business of concordats, need not be discussed here. What is chiefly noteworthy is the line of argument: the laity should exercise their political functions only in obedience to the hierarchy; the clergy must confine themselves to the simple cure of souls—and what this involves is determined by the hierarchy.

SUMMARY

At the end of this 'century of the laity' the official Church in Germany, a novel combination of hierarchs and authoritarian bureaucrats, has, by means of a far-reaching interpretation of basic laws and of its own responsibilities, as well as by a restrictive attitude towards Catholic politicians on the one hand, and towards the political responsibility of priests on the other, succeeded in establishing its claim to exclusive political competence. From questions of the national debt to criminal law reform, from family law to defence policy—over all the Church extends its claim to participate in decision-making. Clergy and laity have the task of being obedient accomplices.

Translated by G. W. S. Knowles

Notes

1. In a long case before the Federal Constitutional Court in 1955-56, the question at issue was the validity of the Reichskonkordat, and whether a federal State (in this case Lower Saxony) could introduce, in the educational field, a new regulation which deviated from the Reichskonkordat. The Court decided that it could, although it explicitly maintained the constitutional validity and continuing legality of the concordat: *Der Konkordatsprozess* ed. v. F. Giese and F. R. Frh. v. d. Heydte (Munich 1957).

2. J. Degen *Diakonie und Restauration. Kritik am sozialen Protestantismus in der Bundesrepublik Deutschland* (Neuwied-Darmstadt 1975) p. 24.

3. *Hirtenbrief der deutschen Bischöfe vom 23.2.1947* (Amtsbl. Rottenburg 19 1947) p. 23.

4. *Hirtenbrief der deutschen Bischöfe vom 28.8.1948* (Amtsbl. Rottenburg 19 1948) pp. 113-116.

5. *ibid.* pp. 195-198

6. W. Wöste 'Die Aufgaben des Katholischen Büros' in G. Gorschenek *Katholiken und ihre Kirche in der Bundesrepublik Deutschland* (Munich-Vienna 1976) pp. 96-104.

7. See, e.g., G. Reidick *Die hierarchische Struktur der Ehe* (Munich 1953); and, in criticism of it, M. Wiedmaier *Die Wertung der Frau in den Hirtenbriefen der deutschen Bischöfe von 1950-59* (typewritten thesis, Tübingen 1978).

8. Quoted in M. Wiedmaier, in the work cited in note 7, pp. 29ff.

9. Amtsbl. Bamberg 1953 pp. 37f.

10. So, e.g., W. Kalisch *Grund- und Einzelfragen des kirchlichen Dienstrechts* (ZEvKR 2, 1952/53) pp. 24ff.

11. Cf. R. Richardi *Kirchenautonomie und gesetzliche Betriebsverfassung* (ZEvKR 23, 1978) pp. 367-413.

12. See J. Neumann 'Demokratie und Normativität. Gegen die Tyrannei der Werte' in *Demokratie im Spektrum der Wissenschaften* ed. K. Hartmann (Frieburg-Munich 1980) pp. 43-107

13. AKathKR 134 (1974) pp. 486-489.

14. See H. Herrmann 'Reichskonkordat unterlaufen?' in *Publik-Forum* of 19.10.1973, p. 19, and K. Walf 'Zur partei-politischen Tätigkeit der Priester' in *Frankfurter Hefte 1974*, pp. 397ff. Against this J. Listl ('Erklärung der deutschen Bischofkonferenz zur parteipolitischen Tätigkeit der Priester' in ÖAKR 26 (1975) pp. 166-176) maintains that the bishops are fully entitled to issue such a declaration.

Jacques Robert

The Political Status and Role of the Churches in France

ONE CANNOT understand the role which the churches in France either play in fact or else hope or fear that they might possibly play in the political life of the nation if one ignores the juridical context within which relationships of power or influence unfold.

Of course France guarantees freedom of religion, but she claims to be 'neutral'. She regards herself as 'secular', 'lay', which means to say that she will neither 'recognise' nor 'assist' the religions. What, therefore, are the implications of such a situation as far as the political position which the churches could be led to adopt on this or that problem is concerned?

1. THE COMPLEX NATURE OF RELIGIOUS FREEDOM

Religious freedom is a complex reality, in which it is possible to discern three distinct elements.

It consists in the first place in the affirmation that each one must be free to give his intellectual assent or not to this or that religion—and by religion must be understood any belief, any faith, any explanation or vision of the world, any conception of the universe, and indeed any community of shared feeling or life.[1] In this sense, religious freedom amounts to a freedom of opinion: it is freedom of conscience.

But religious freedom is much more than that. It cannot simply be considered as freedom of opinion, the fact being that the religious reality is not limited to a belief, a faith. All religions, all sects, and all schools of thought involve, in addition to a body of doctrine to which the believer, follower or militant gives his assent, the observance of rites, in short a cult. The observance of the cult, which often calls at the outset for a ritual initiation and subsequently assumes fidelity to customs and traditions, and even to an individual pattern of life based on regular exercises, is, from the point of view of the believer, a fundamental aspect of religion and not simply a way of expressing religious belief. Religious freedom, therefore, can only exist in so far as a second element—freedom of worship—is added to freedom of conscience.

This obviously presupposes a third element: the freedom of the churches to organise themselves. Most religions in fact possess an organisational framework, a church, though the degree of organisation of each one is different. Some are hierarchically

53

structured on a world scale; others are merely national; while others still prefer to give the 'grass-roots' greater independence and provide only organs of co-ordination. The range, which passes from the Roman Catholic Church, via the national churches or federations, to certain regional sects, is particularly varied. But what is essential is that each church should have the right to establish itself freely and to live and act as it wishes—in conformity, that is, with an inner law that it has laid down for itself. One cannot demand of a church that it conform to a uniform and pre-established pattern.

Does this mean that within the national collectivity the churches would constitute worlds apart, States within the State? That there would exist within a single State two codes of law, one 'civil' to regulate individual and collective behaviour in an exclusively temporal universe, the other 'religious' to set the pace for the life of the recognised churches? The problem of religious freedom is not limited to the idea of the freedom of the churches. It is also necessarily going to emerge in the context of relations between the churches and the State.

2. THE LEGAL SEPARATION OF CHURCH AND STATE

Having in the course of her history tried every possible formula, from the State religion to concordatory arrangements, and including the recognition of cults and the publicisation or 'Frenchification' of the churches, France settled in 1905 for the 'separation' of Church and State.

This desire, ratified by the law of 1905, not to recognise religious cults officially does not imply that the Republic disregards the existence in France of several great religions. The Republic simply affirms that she is henceforth abandoning the system of recognised religions, and therefore eliminating all distinction between the 'official' religions and the rest—putting them all on the same level. It no longer 'recognises' them but rather 'knows' them.

This absence of recognition does not, moreover, signify that the State does not wish to maintain a relationship of trust with the religions: it is simply saying that, contrary to what the concordatory solutions would suggest, religion is no longer a public matter. For all that it remains no less a 'social' matter.

What is certain, however, is that no French juridical text any longer officially accepts the existence of cults or religions. Indeed, one can ask whether our law as a whole has not obliterated all trace of God.

At the constitutional level, first of all, one is struck by the fact that nowhere in our present charter is the word 'cult' mentioned, and that 'religion' is invoked only in the course of Article 2. 'France', this article stipulates, 'assures all citizens of equality before the law, without distinction of origin, race or religion.' It makes clear in the same way that the Republic respects all forms of belief.

This double guarantee of equality and freedom completes the affirmation of the lay nature of the State. It is in fact in the first paragraph of the same Article that our country is described as an 'indivisible, lay, democratic and social Republic'.

Our constitution evidently does no more than spell out laconically the consequences of this secularity.

In this respect, it is interesting to note that the draft constitution of 19 April 1946 was more prolix. One reads in fact in Article 13 of the Declaration of Human Rights that precedes this text not only that 'no one can be harassed on account of his origins, of his opinions or beliefs in religious, philosophical or political matters', but that 'freedom is guaranteed, notably by the separation of the churches from the State, as well as by the lay character of the government and of State education'.

This reference to the separation of the powers was left out of the 1946 text, and of that of 1958. In the latter, however, it is stated right from the start that the French people is solemnly committed to human rights and to the principles of national sovereignty as these were defined by the Declaration of 1789, and confirmed and completed by the preamble to the Constitution of 1946.

This threefold reference permits one to infer at the juridical level that the stipulations included in the texts mentioned must be considered to have constitutional value. At the religious level, therefore, this means that no one can be harassed on account of his opinions; that the fundamental principles recognised by the laws of the Republic—the principles, that is, that were laid down through the great liberal laws of the Third Republic, and notably, in so far as we are concerned here, the separation of Church and State and freedom of education—must be respected; and finally that a certain number of State services, for example the organisation of free, non-religious public education, should be considered as 'particularly necessary for our time'.

The 1958 Constitution therefore in no way rejects the 'lay' achievement of the preceding republics, and it adopts freedom of conscience. But it limits itself to recalling this fidelity without feeling the need to insist on it further.

Religion, therefore, seems truly to have become exterior to the State. It no longer appears as anything more than the manifestation of a private freedom, every element of public right having truly disappeared. A lay State, therefore, is one which stands outside any form of religious obedience and which refuses the status of public right to each and every form of religious activity.

3. THE POLITICAL SIGNIFICANCE OF THE SEPARATION OF CHURCH AND STATE

The question of Church-State relations is not limited, moreover, to the mere search for and choice of the most suitable formula. In a much more general way, it poses the problem of the respective political attitudes which, over and above the law, the churches and the State are going to decide to have between them.

The true debate takes place, in fact, at the level of their coexistence. The question is whether it is possible for a lay State, responsible for the destiny of all its citizens, whatever their religion, to coexist with churches that are entirely free in their decisions.

It has rightly been said that 'the drama of the Christian—even when he claims to be a citizen of the world—is that he has two fatherlands: that of his passport and that of his baptism. Such a man is born divided. . . .'[2]

How, in their turn, should the churches not be divided too? Guardians of a message which it is their *raison d'être* to announce to the world, how will they manage to remain faithful to the 'great hope' while having of necessity to insert themselves into the political structures which threaten, if not to stifle them, at least to compromise them?

The problem is, in fact, twofold. In the first place there is the question of the position that the churches cannot but adopt with regard to the serious questions of modern ethics, given that the faithful expect them to pronounce on these and offer guidance. And then there is the overall attitude which the churches must adopt to the government.

4. CHANGING RELATIONSHIPS BETWEEN CHURCH AND STATE

There is certainly no 'confessional party' in France, which is to say that there is no political grouping which claims to be or recognises itself as the product of a church or a religion. Christians are to be found at every point of the political spectrum; they are divided among all the parties. This does not mean that there is no Catholic, Protestant or Jewish feeling about this or that question. But the diversity of the Christian electorate make hierarchies cautious.

E

Of course there are some questions on which it is scarcely conceivable that certain churches could compromise. It is taken for granted in France that the Catholic Church will publicly condemn abortion, refuse to accept divorce, remain cautious about questions as delicate as artificial insemination or *in vitro* fertilisation and come out in favour of conscientious objection. No one expects her to repudiate her message, even when she is aware that people have unconsciously abandoned it. Other churches will be more liberal on these particular points.

But all stand shoulder to shoulder in France to defend the rights and freedoms of the human person, since it is man, this being created in the image of God, who must be protected first and foremost—protected against arbitrary arrest and detention, ill-treatment and torture; and protected, too, against hunger, loneliness, despair, war and death. In other words, it is necessary to work above all for peace among men through the rapprochement of peoples and nations.

Should the Church preach in the wilderness, or should she take the opportunity to accept government assistance if it is offered, without paying too much attention to the methods used by the government?

On their side, the Christians of France have never been the natural allies of political power. The State has never inspired them with great confidence. Because it is, without a doubt, difficult to belong to two different worlds, and to reconcile two concerns, because what is 'to come' is more important than what is happening 'at present', Christians have not always put up very easily with the State. But formerly, even if they did not like it, they reckoned that as arbiter of the common good it was serving the general interest, and their churches saw to it that they did not make things difficult for it and even supported it. Even though this alliance between the government and the Church has never been more than 'circumstantial', it has nevertheless existed—and for a long time. Does official language not speak of the 'civil, military and religious authorities'?[3]

If the separation—'anti-clerical' or 'irreligious' idea!—was effected juridically in France in 1905, all the efforts of Roman Catholicism since then have tended towards the re-establishment of the links. Thus the image of the Church which many people still preserve is of a monolithic and powerful institution, the guardian of order and the 'unbiased ally' of the government.

Today, however, it seems that the Church is emancipating itself, even rebelling. If the State is experienced increasingly as an instrument of oppression, to maintain relations with it is to betray the oppressed. The churches are becoming ever more aware that their 'credibility' depends above all on the resolution and consistency with which they pursue their defence of the oppressed and the victims of injustice. The image of a reassuring Church, preaching resignation to the poor in exchange for a better life is no longer appreciated. And what is more, has not revolution made a discreet entry into the world of believers? The view is gaining currency that, in order to fulfil her mission of evangelisation, the Church has no need to have recourse to means which would make it dependent on the civil authorities, and that, her role being essentially spiritual, to agree to take her place in the social pageant is to betray her mission.[4]

It is in the light of the churches' growing awareness of the subdued rumblings that are rising up from the 'marginalised' that one should interpret the kind of 'notice' which the Catholic Church and the Protestant Federation in France seem increasingly to want to give to the civil authorities through declarations or publications which condemn particular initiatives or undertakings of the government.

But does this institutional protest perhaps not run the risk of substituting a political messianism for the messianism of the gospel? And in wishing not to be associated with the government, is the Church not becoming in her turn an anti-authority?

It is difficult for churchmen to pass on a non-temporal message. The word of God is present and actual or it dies. How then can they avoid adopting a position on all the problems of our time?

The essential thing is that they should do it with moderation and objectivity, in order to avoid being reproached some day for having sought to impose on a Republic that is profoundly secular the possibly out-dated principles of a Christianity in decline.

Translated by Sarah Fawcett

Notes

1. See A. de Laubadère *Cours de Droit public 1953-1954* (Paris, Les Cours de Droit) pp. 289ff.; G. Burdeau *Les Libertés publiques* (Paris, Librairie générale de Droit et de Jurisprudence 1972) p. 341; C. A. Colliard *Libertés publiques* (Dalloz 1975) p. 353; Jacques Robert *Libertés publiques* (Paris 1971) pp. 324ff.; Jacques Robert *La Liberté religieuse et le régime des cultes* (Paris 1977).

2. Henri Fesquet *Le Monde*, 2 August 1974.

3. See: René Rémond 'Eglise et Etat: vers une seconde séparation?' *Projet* (April 1972) 445.

4. See: Mgr Huygue 'L'Eglise fait de la politique' *La Croix*, 18 March 1972.

Hans-Hermann Hücking

The Political Role of the
Official Church in Hungary

THE OFFICIALLY structured Catholic Church of Hungary remains a national institution bound to a State bureaucracy that describes itself as socialist and for which it provides partial legitimation. But this verdict on the interplay of two so unequal forces, a verdict that will find its detailed justification in what follows, is reduced by historical perspective to merely a new variant of the fact of the proclamation of the gospel and State power having for centuries gone hand in hand in the history of institutional Christianity. Hence it only makes credible sense to criticise without denouncing the voluntary or involuntary legitimation by the Church of the repressive structures of State-established socialism if this takes place in the light of a new critical ecclesiology of the Church as a whole and leads to a process of fundamental self-criticism with regard to the Church and its relationship to the power of the State.

The Catholic Church in Hungary as a sociologically tangible social institution—represented by the episcopate and to a certain extent by the 'Catholic Committee of the National Peace Council' (OBKB)[1]—has for the past thirty years expressed itself in an intensely and explicitly politicised terminology which leaves the well-founded impression of a variant of classical political theology that gave the power of the State additional legitimation. Quite apart from whether the context of such verbal approval is primarily defined by opportunist motives, tactical considerations or genuine convictions, the Hungarian Church's function of political affirmation should not be reduced to this alone nor even to this primarily. The real ecclesiological problem is not the public politicised language, the effect of which on the faithful should in no way be over-estimated, but the Church's leading political function, which leads to highly dubious consequences primarily within the Church: the extent to which, in exchange for concessions on the part of the State that are justified from the religious point of view and are substantial from the point of view of traditional ecclesiology, its leadership is ready in the policies and strategies it adopts to become the defenders and accomplices of the internal political interests and measures of the State's social system.[2]

1. THE CHURCH AS AN ORGAN OF LEGITIMATION FOR THE STATE

A few examples selected from recent history will verify the thesis that the Hungarian episcopate's public statements on the relationship of Church and State must be read and understood directly and immediately as supporting and stabilising the system:

(*a*) On the thirtieth anniversary of the agreement between Church and State the bishops' conference published a statement entitled 'Sharing in Building up the Country'. In conformity with the humiliating conditions for the Church under which this agreement came into being, this statement has a consistently conformist and servile tone: 'In 1950 the conditions for the rebirth (of the new nation) were already visible: all power was now possessed by the working people'—although precisely in this period of Stalinism, which even officially in Hungary today is criticised as the time of the 'cult of personality', Cardinal Mindszenty was condemned to life-imprisonment at a show trial and many priests and hundreds of religious were imprisoned. The document goes on to assure its readers that 'a good mutual relationship exists between the State and the Church. . . . Today we can say with assurance that we are following a successful path'.[2] The statement does not mention either the overt or covert regimentation of the Church over the past thirty years or the still unsolved questions and the justified demands of Hungarian Catholics for unrestricted freedom of religion and conscience.

(*b*) The State marked this thirtieth anniversary by on 30 August 1980 awarding four bishops the highest State decoration, the banner of the Hungarian People's Republic. The award of this decoration, which had previously often been bestowed on bishops and priests of the OBKB, shows in itself a form of close co-operation with the State that is highly questionable from the point of view of the Church's political role. The speeches given on this occasion had the function of demonstrating an amicable relationship between Church and State. Thus the Prime Minister, György Lázár, pointed to the 'harmonious development' of mutual relations during the thirty years since the agreement was signed. Cardinal László Lékai confirmed this, though he did mention, even if in very euphemistic terms, the 'initial oppression' that the Church had had to endure. The path on which the Church could now continue 'step by step' had not been 'covered with carpets and strewn with flowers'. Difficult and painful work had been needed so that the agreement could develop into a stable basis on which they could confidently build in the future.

(*c*) The legitimation of the social system (and its treatment of the Church) by representatives of the Church itself does not take place only within the country's borders. Thus in an interview with the Italian Catholic periodical *Il Regno* Cardinal Lékai asserted that in Hungary Marxism had been able to realise the injunctions of the social encyclical *Quadragesimo anno*, whereas in the rest of the Catholic world the realisation of these papal directives had not yet taken place. To prove this the cardinal quoted the fact that peasants were doing well in Hungary and that medical treatment was free for everyone (and thus for priests too), while pensions were provided for everybody.[3]

(*d*) Typical are the statements made by the episcopate in March 1981 to mark the seventh congress of the Hungarian Patriotic Popular Front.[4] The statement of the bishops' conference gave positive approval to the co-operation of the various forces of society in the context of the Popular Front. The working programme was guided by the idea of national unity and brought 'wide sections of society together': 'The co-operation of the Catholic Church and the Popular Front can be significant and fruitful because the Church is given ever greater guarantees for the free contribution of its moral powers in the interest of the realisation of the great social and at the same time political goals of the fatherland.' They should continue to follow the path they had so far been taking: 'We offer the Popular Front our co-operation.' The response of the first secretary of the Hungarian Socialist Workers' Party, János Kádár, was that relations with the churches were good. The representatives of the churches respected the constitution and would help the people to build up a socialist society and a better future for the nation. In return the State respected 'the churches' freedom of conscience and their autonomy'. At the same time 'national unity' was urged as an 'essential part of the socialist system'.[5]

The empty formula of 'national unity', however, is merely the label hiding the political system's aim of containing within a pre-determined framework all ideological forces opposed to Marxism-Leninism, such as the churches. In this context the relationship with the churches aimed at by the Party is based on two principles: mutual toleration on the one hand, on the other strict separation of Church and State. For the most part both principles have remained ideals, even if they are presented by State propaganda as having been realised. The Party and government present the separation of Church and State in Hungary as one of the historically most progressive solutions; but in practice it is accompanied by the attempt to insinuate a far-reaching liaison of interests between State and Church in social and political questions, particularly with regard to internal and external politics. The formula 'constructive and held in an atmosphere of mutual trust' is used to describe the conversations which the State department for religious affairs hold with the Church—always behind closed doors and always only with the Church leadership. The desire for 'relationships of partnership' hides the aim of having at one's disposal a Church that is firmly controlled and can be counted on politically, and of clearing up nascent conflicts without their coming to public attention at all.

Quite apart from whether the bishops' statements on social and political questions are made under compulsion or voluntarily, they are confined exclusively to statements on subjects approved by the State such as questions of security, disarmament, the normalisation of relations between Church and State. They are expressions of classical 'political theology' inasmuch as they repeat political options put into currency from another source and indicate the Church's agreement with them.

Although several bishops fairly consistently adopt anti-socialist positions in private as far as their social and political views are concerned, when it comes to statements issued to the faithful and confidential discussions with the State department for religious affairs they are prepared to become defenders of the political interests and decisions of the socialism that actually exists. But in any case they are not cynical hirelings of an oppressive power, as they are occasionally presented in the West, but rather partners in the business of maintaining public order.[6] But both this order and the allegedly good relations between Church and State are threatened by the small grass-roots groups that have sprung up among Catholics.[7]

2. THE ALLIANCE OF STATE AND CHURCH AGAINST GRASS-ROOTS GROUPS

(a) The position of the State authorities

The Hungarian security forces regard every informal religious association, as well as non-religious ones, as having a politically subversive character if and because they do not appear transparent enough to the authorities and cannot thus come under their direct control. Behind every collective endeavour of this kind the party sees tendencies that it describes as 'hostile to the State' or indeed 'counter-revolutionary'.

Up until early 1976 even Catholic grass-roots groups were subject to police persecution. They were accused of illegal organisation, conspiracy, or preparing to overthrow State order, and severe penalties were inflicted on their members. The charges could, however, never be proved: rather what was continually demonstrated was that these groups were concerned only with questions of the religious life.

In 1976, following the publication of the international convention regarding the civil and political rights established by the United Nations,[8] a change occurred in the State's treatment of these grass-roots groups in the form of an 'edict of toleration'. At the same time the State expected the newly appointed Primate Archbishop Lékai, as the responsible leader of the Hungarian Church, to observe the 1950 agreement under which the bishops' conference was assigned the duty 'of proceeding according to the Church's jurisdiction against Church personnel who act against the legal order of the Hungarian People's Republic and against the government's work of reconstruction'. The State's attitude was now that the Church's field of activity had undergone an expansion with the recognition of the ecclesial character of these grass-roots groups but that at the same time it must bear responsibility for them. Thus on the transparent pretext of not wanting to intervene 'in the internal affairs of the bishops' function of leadership' the State department of religious affairs provided Cardinal Lékai in December 1976 with a list of the priests who co-operated with these groups.[9] This also explains why Secretary of State Imre Miklós, when asked about the existence of these grass-roots groups at a press conference in Rome on 9 October 1980, answered briefly that this was not his concern nor that of the State but of the Church.

(b) The position of the episcopate

As long as the State persecuted these grass-roots groups as hostile to the State they did not amount to any significant problem for the official Church. But after the State, at least in its official statements, had declared them to belong to the Church and had assigned them to the sphere of competence of the Church's leadership, conflicts arose within the Church. The bishops based their objections to the grass-roots groups not on the duty of oversight attributed to them by the State but appealed instead to their apostolic office. Quite apart from their desire to avoid any tension with the State authorities, and particularly when what was involved were in the eyes of the State opposition groups, their major difficulties clearly arose above all from the way in which these grass-roots groups threatened to call the bishops' claim to leadership into question.

In spite of all the theological statements and disciplinary measures which from 1976 onwards the bishops applied against these groups, the conflict was dramatically intensified when a member of one of these groups refused military service on conscientious grounds and in September 1976 was condemned by a Hungarian court. When the groups urged the bishops' conference to appeal to the State for the introduction of a non-combatant social alternative to military service, they were accused of agitation and incitement. It is in this context that we must see the suspension and forced assignment to a particular place of the two priests László Kovács and András Gromon in the autumn of 1981.

According to a statement by Cardinal Lékai, Kovács was suspended not only because he maintained contacts with grass-roots groups active outside the hierarchy's sphere of responsibility but also because he personally defended some of their views that could not be reconciled with the teaching of the Church. In addition Kovács was alleged to have explicitly encouraged young Christians to refuse military service.[10]

Pacifist tendencies among young Christians were also the subject of strong criticism from the secretary of the OBKB and Member of Parliament Canon Imre Biró: 'Love of one's country means protecting one's country', he said, and this was something one must learn within the framework of military service. Young people must learn to fit in to the existing order and to obey orders.[11]

In this way the State leaves it to the bishops and to the priests organised in the OBKB to adopt clear standpoints with regard to the extremely subversive calling into question of military service. The attitude of the official Church in this context confirms once again the conviction of the grass-roots groups and of a growing number of priests[12] that the leadership of the Church cannot be looked to in order to proclaim the gospel in accordance with the needs of the time and in a way that takes into account people's social and personal problems in Hungary. A precondition for this would be the leaders of the Hungarian Church saying good-bye to all politico-theological options and policy strategies that do more to help the survival of the Church as an institution than the life of the Church community as a whole. This would involve the bishops refusing to endorse State domestic and foreign policy and their explicit rejection of the function ascribed to them by the State of judging movements of renewal within the Church from the point of view of their possible effect on the political system and then stifling these by administrative measures.

Translated by Robert Nowell

Notes

1. The peace priests' movement, known since 1956 as the Catholic Committee of the National Peace Council (OBKB), was founded in Hungary in 1950 on the Czechoslovak model. The committee is integrated into the Patriotic Popular Front and is meant to intervene actively on behalf of the regime's policy with regard to the Church and peace among the country's Catholics, acting as a transmitter for the State department of religious affairs. Three priests belonging to the OBKB are members of the Budapest Parliament. The OBKB supports the aims of the World Peace Council directed by the USSR and co-operates closely with analogous groups of priests and lay-people in other East European countries.

2. Katholische Nachrichten-Agentur, Bonn, 28 August 1980.

3. *Il Regno* no. 20, 1980, quoted from *Frankfurter Allgemeine Zeitung*, 22 November 1980.

4. The Patriotic Popular Front sees itself as a joint political platform for all social organisations and institutions in Hungary, with representatives of the religious communities taking part in its work at all levels from the local to the national.

5. Kathpress, Vienna, no. 54, 19 March 1981.

6. Ferenc Fehér '"Kadarismus": Analyse des tolerantesten Blocklandes Osteuropas' in F. Fehér and A. Heller *Diktatur über die Bedürfnisse* (Hamburg 1979) 146-147.

7. See Hans-Hermann Hücking 'Katholische Basisgruppen in Ungarn', in *Kirche von Unten. Alternative Gemeinden* ed. Hubert Frankemölle (Mainz/Munich 1981) pp. 189-211.

8. Legal regulation no. 8, 1976.

9. Many of the priests named were suddenly transferred to other parishes early in 1977. Some of them have since left Hungary or asked for laicisation.

10. Kathpress, Vienna, no. 184, 24 September 1981.

11. Kathpress, Vienna, no. 208, 29 October 1981.

12. In an open letter to Cardinal Lékai dated 19 November 1981, a group of priests accused him of adopting a position other than that of the Council, which explicitly recognised the right of conscientious objection to military service. The suspension of Fathers Kovács and Gromon showed that the Church was not taking any notice of current problems and was condemning 'with the methods of the middle ages those that take a different view'. The letter added: 'We cannot understand why the head of the Hungarian Church breaks a lance for the military authorities. . . . In our view the Hungarian bishops should in this difficult time follow the same path as the Evangelical Church in the German Democratic Republic, which finds itself in an even more difficult situation.'

Jan Heijke

Church and State in Africa

THE SUBJECT 'Church and State in Africa' is a very broad one and has still been the object of very little systematic study. Without doubt this is owing to the fact that the embodiment of the concept of 'State' in the Black continent is not yet stable. *Coups d'état* occur with considerable frequency there and in some countries there is still conflict regarding the setting of territorial boundaries. In most countries a one-party system prevails, while the government of some countries might be called dictatorial. In South Africa the State represents only the advantaged white minority of the population. Besides capitalist-oriented countries there are several which have opted for some form of socialism or other.

From the quantity of possibilities I have chosen merely one, one aspect that is common to many African countries. Most States are young. They see themselves confronted by the task of making an integrated modern society, a nation, out of an economically independent rural population. What is the Church's role in this?

1. YOUNG STATES

In the precolonial period in Africa there were leaders and intertribal relations. In the colonial period the fabric of overseas European government policy was superimposed on this, into which the precolonial inter-ethnic and intra-ethnic power relationships nevertheless did not completely dissolve. Moreover, in both periods it was true that the grip of a central authority on the extended families within a self-sufficiency economy was much weaker than in our western countries.

When present-day African countries became independent they inherited the arbitrary territorial borders which had been drawn by the colonial political cartographers. But when people speak of African States, for them the word State has the same meaning it has if, for example, Sweden or France is under discussion. In a workshop on African studies experts (December 1981, Leiden) a paper was presented with the significant title 'Is Chad still a State?'[1]. Indeed, when can one call a society a State? That is not just an academic question. That international recognition, for example by means of representation in the UN or in the Organisation for African Unity, is not the only or even the main factor in answering this question, is obvious. A certain degree of national integration is indispensable if the State is not to be a fiction. If this integration is disrupted by civil war, by a long-lasting disruption of communications

63

between the regions and the centre of government or the military high command, by disintegration of the national economy and of the monetary unit, the postcolonial artificial country can perhaps still save its face before the international community for a considerable time, but one might wonder whether it still deserves the name of State. Chad is at the moment the clearest example of such a disintegration, although some other young African States are also in a shaky condition: we need only think of Angola, Ethiopia or Uganda. That the long birth-pangs of the State of Angola have forced the episcopate to adopt a different attitude towards the national government from that which the Church adopts or can adopt in Mozambique, is clear.

2. WEAK LEGITIMACY

But those African countries which have found their own identity since their independence and for whom it would appear that the concept of nation can be applied with more confidence, are also experiencing at this very point of national formation problems which industrialised countries elsewhere in the world do not have. A highly praised recent study on Tanzania[2] has drawn attention to the dogged resistance put up by the so-called relationship economy—also called the 'peasant economy' or 'economy of affection'—against merging into a great whole that can then be called nation. By relationship or peasant economy is understood the method of production of (pre-industrial) agrarian societies, or rather, of families which—barring unforeseen disasters such as floods or long-lasting drought—are independent of aid from outside for their existence. Reproduction and maintenance of the family, not production, is of primary importance in agriculture and handicrafts. The size of the land brought under cultivation and the level of production are closely related to the needs of the extended family. As long as there is no shortage of agricultural land these agrarian families are practically immune from attempts at integration by a self-imposed central authority (colonial or post-colonial). In the eyes of these families a State coming from above can make no claim on their support. 'The public realm lacks legitimacy in Africa', says Hyden, looking beyond Tanzania to Black Africa in general.[3] But without supra-familial provisions a modern State cannot exist, nor without officials (government functionaries and experts) and people who hire out their labour. These wage-earners must be fed via additional work from the rural population. In return for this additional work the State can then supply the necessary services for the development of the country as a whole. Via a 'surplus extraction'[4] the national authority will thus have to breach the self-sufficiency economy and graft on or incorporate it into the expanding national economy.

Two factors immediately present us with ticklish problems. First, how, in a situation of national formation, does the central authority come about? In a fragmented self-sufficiency society the national authority does not arise from below, but rather happens to the rural population. The loud cheers on the transfer of sovereignty on Independence Day should mislead no one: the legitimacy of the national government in the young African countries is quite peculiar to those countries, and not the same as that of the State authorities in settled European nations. On behalf of whom does this central government speak in the African countries? Words like 'people's republic' or slogans like 'Tout pour le Peuple! Rien que pour le Peuple!' do not alter the fact that even socialist African heads of State are still not the exponents of people's power. They exert themselves to instil their socialism into the people, but these are options from on high. And this introduces a second factor which presents outsiders and those involved with knotty problems: the integration of a self-sufficiency economy into a national economy cannot occur without compulsion. This compulsion intervenes radically in the life of the people and causes a lot of distress. The State in Black Africa is therefore a weakly legitimised authority[5] which has to incorporate the agrarian population by force into a nascent nation.

But the State is not composed only of the head of State; it also comprises an apparatus of officials and experts, themselves coming from the rural population with their relationship-economy. Education or training do not seem adequate to detach these people sufficiently from their family bonds. For the conscience of those concerned, as well as in public opinion (and letters sent in to the local press notwithstanding), the demands of the relationship-economy are often more highly regarded than the national interest. The concept of responsibility among officials is still often not attuned to the national economy. As long as land is not scarce and officials or party leaders still have the possibility of falling back on their home village, they are relatively immune to sanctions from the central authority. These are the people who must wield State authority and must carry through the compulsion needed in order to build up the nation. That this offers the possibility of an uneven distribution of distress is clear.

Although the picture drawn here is valid for a large part of Black Africa, there are variations and the State may be less weakly anchored in one country or region than in another. But the meshing-in of the independent, self-supporting rural population into a large-scale system such as that of a modern nation is a task which the authorities of many African States still largely have to tackle. In a survey of the relation between Church and politics in Africa, therefore, a definition of the position of the State must be included in any considerations.

Before I make a few remarks on the role of the Church in the African countries I should like—perhaps superfluously—to make the point that it is impossible to separate politics from economics, and furthermore that it is impossible to separate politics and economics from cultural and ethical values. To bring a rural population which chooses to paddle its own canoe on board the ship of State means a profound intervention in the universe of meaning of that population. Fundamental values like family (extended family) and marriage are at issue here. Whether Church leaders and officials are explicitly aware of their political role or not, their pastoral influence is bound up with the national destiny of the population.

The Church represents a force in Black Africa. By virtue of their numbers, its adherents are a factor which must be taken into account in any efforts at forming a nation. The close connections of the churches in Africa with Europe and North America give them a lot of financial scope which is applied to a not insignificant degree in social provisions such as education, health care and development projects. They are tightly organised, with a hierarchy at national level and pastors who, in comparison with those of Islam or of the traditional religion, are very well grounded. Even if the government apparatus founders and all sorts of services stagnate, the 'mission posts' carry on functioning: a factor of stability in the region.[6] In countries where the State authority or the party has a monopoly over the corporate life, the churches remain as the only alternative opinion-forming enclaves. In short, the Church in Africa has a political dimension and therefore plays a part in the integration of the society into a nation. Where in Africa the State authority is only weakly anchored in the fragmented society, the supportive or contesting position of the Church is all the more important. In such a situation a number of elements can be discerned in the role of the Church.

3. PRODUCTIVIST CIVILISATION?

The most fundamental political question on which the Church should concentrate seems to me to be this: In this agrarian society, on what basis must the way to modernisation, i.e., to entry into a large-scale growth economy, be taken? A good deal of the choices of the national government stand or fall with the answer to this question. It is not realistic to leave such a fundamental question unasked, although everyone is swayed by the number of obvious advantages which modernisation brings, and although it is certain that the mass of the African population would opt for the material blessings of a growth economy. Cardinal Razafimahatrata of Madagascar's pastoral letter of 27 July 1980 acknowledges his realisation of this problem when he mentions 'questions which are the result of the choice in favour of a productivist civilisation and which could have been prevented if account had been taken of certain cultural values'.[7] This fundamental question is all the more urgent not only because a choice between methods of production is being made, but because the universe of meaning is at stake. Only for very weighty reasons may the security which this universe of meaning offers be attacked.[8] Although it is true that man—whether western or African—is no longer sitting in the 'driver's seat' and history seems to be pursuing its own course, going on outside him as it were, he nevertheless remains challenged to oppose it.

4. LEGITIMATE CONTRIBUTION

A second element concerns the legitimacy of the State in Africa. The State can and will, under certain conditions, be regarded as an advance guard of the population on the path to formation as a nation. It is not the voice of the people, but the voice towards the people. In so far as the local church underwrites the concrete aims of the country concerned it must also consciously place its legitimate capacities at the service of national formation. It is true that nation and population do not yet coincide, nor may State and nation be identified with one another. Therefore the legitimisation which the Church can give will always have a provisional character. That does not mean that it must keep itself aloof until the State leadership has succeeded in becoming the true representation of the population. Under the influence of Latin American literature, some Tanzanian priests have thought they could offer material for an indigenous theology of liberation.[9] The function of such a liberation theology should, however, be that of a legitimate support in order to help the weakly anchored government to find a better reception among the Christian part of the population, while the function of the Latin American model is that of a prophetic protest.

5. PROTESTING FUNCTION

That brings me to a third element: the attitude of the Church towards the compulsion which is indispensable if the population is to be transformed into a nation. An extremely delicate point. For in the resistance of the rural population is hidden, not primarily backwardness, but a deeply-rooted cultural sense of values. The ideal, endorsed by many, that the population itself must be the subject, not the object of change, deserves the greatest attention. Nevertheless compulsion is unavoidable. That this compulsion can assume drastic forms is shown by the attempts in Mozambique and Tanzania at a regrouping of the rural population. In the latter country 9·5 million people were involved in this gigantic shift of the population (1973-76). In judging the legitimacy of force the Church will have to be aware both of her legitimising (and in this sense also mitigating) and of her contesting function. The point of departure in this must be that the suffering is to be kept to the minimum, must be distributed as fairly as possible and must be in proportion to the real chances of an actual improvement in destiny. The longer the period foreseen between the carrying out of the painful compulsion and the realisation of the hoped for favourable result on behalf of the population, the greater the considerations must be. Moreover the Church will have to see to it, using all the means at her command, that the population is heard, that dissidents consequently can express their views on how the nation is built. A sensitive point, as in Africa the ruling party often entertains an idea of loyalty which is not based on principles or political views but on personal association. Moreover, the party tends to present itself as all-embracing. Any opposition, any alternative, therefore, is quickly regarded as treason.[10] It is the task of the Church in Africa to let the voices of those who are suffering most filter upwards.

What form a protest must assume in the given circumstances in order to be effective is partly defined by the impact of the oral culture with its own means of communication. Efficient protests do not then always need to have a legalistic character. Yet the published reports of, for example, a Church organisation such as *Justitia et Pax*, in the former Rhodesia, proved extremely effective,[11] and much is also expected of the organisation of the same name in modern Tanzania. Pastoral episcopal letters are also used as a means to expose negative situations, such as in North Cameroon (1980) or in Zaïre (1981). Elsewhere the withholding of legitimate support can be a telling form of protest, though a protest which, it is true, escapes the attention of foreign observers. I am thinking here of the absence of open Church protest in the Central African Republic under Bokassa, although one might wonder whether at the imperial coronation the Church could have played a different role from that which she in fact fulfilled at the time. Protesting comes more easily to a prophet than to an institution. Playing safe for the sake of the facilities which the Church enjoys as a social institution can prove restricting.

Protest and legitimising can go together. Protest may be registered against the blunt or ill-prepared way in which a compulsory measure which is in itself unavoidable is carried out, while the measure as a whole is approved. I cite again an example from Tanzania. The 'villagisation' of the rural population was an extremely tough measure. The Church more than once registered objections against locally irresponsible actions. Yet there is a correlation between protest and legitimisation. Protest will be more effective to the degree in which the Church lets her legitimising role appear not only in words but also in deeds. President Nyerere has repeatedly stressed this to the clergy, with little success, by stating that they should also settle in the new villages in order to take part in agriculture. Here he has pointed out how lightly Islam travels: a religion without presbyteries and without paid religious leaders.[12] In Mozambique a part of the African clergy has recognised the positive importance of handicrafts and wage-earning.[13] A tangibly manifested solidarity doubtless as gives a greater right to the expression of criticism.

That the fulfilling of their political task means for the Church in Africa an investment demanding sacrifices is true both where the letigimising and the contesting factors are concerned.

Notes

1. R. Buijtenhuijs 'Is Tsjaad nog een staat?' paper presented to the African Studies Centre, Leiden, 1981, 5 pp.

2. Goran Hyden *Beyond Ujamaa in Tanzania. Underdevelopment and an Uncaptured Peasantry* (London 1980). See also: P. P. Rey *Capitalisme négrier: la marche des paysans vers le prolétariat* (Paris 1976).

4. Joinet states that for Tanzania this additional labour must come to 40 per cent. See Bernard Joinet *Tanzanie. Manger d'abord* (Paris 1981) p. 43.

5. David Apter 'Non-western government and politics' in *Comparative Politics* (Free Press 1963) speaks of 'weak legitimacy' or 'weakly legitimised' (pp. 647-649).

6. Maurice Ahanhanzo Glélé *Religion, culture et politique en Afrique noire* (Paris 1981) pp. 187-188.

7. Pastoral letter: 'Engagement chrétien dans la vie nationale', *Foie et Développement* No. 79 (Aug.-Sept. 1980): 'Many of these problems, which are the result of a choice for a productivist civilisation shared by the industrialised countries, whether socialist or capitalist, could have been avoided if certain cultural values which characterise our national identity had been taken into account' (p. 3).

8. P. L. Berger *Les Mystificateurs du progrès* (Paris 1978) ch. VI: 'La politique et le calcul du sens' (pp. 200-226), emphasises the need to respect this universe of meaning (original English title: *Pyramids of Sacrifice* (New York 1974)).

9. See L. Magesa 'Towards a theology of liberation for Tanzania' in E. Fasholé-Luke *Christianity in Independent Africa* (London 1978) p. 514.

10. Lucian W. Pye 'The non-western political process' in *Comparative Politics* eds. H. Eckstein and David Apter (New York 1963) pp. 657-659.

11. Edna McDonagh *The Demands of Simple Justice* (Dublin 1980) p. 101.

12. Jan P. van Bergen *Development and Religion in Tanzania*. Sociological soundings on Christian participation in rural transformation (Madras and Interuniversity Institute for Missiology, Leiden 1981) pp. 329-330.

13. *A New People, a New Church? Mozambique* ('s-Hertogenbosch 1977) p. 120.

Fernando Cardenal

The Political Role of Ministers of the Catholic Church in Nicaragua

INTRODUCTION

THIS IS not going to be a theological treatise, but a piece of testimony. There has been a lot written on the place of priests in politics. I think the most valuable contribution I can make to the subject is through an account of my own experience. Here, our choices have been made as a result of the questions and challenges posed by the particular history of our countries and only a knowledge of that history can lead to an understanding of our position.

Our Christian commitment has several starting-points:

(1) I start from the basis that the people of God and the mass of the people, the poor, have in Latin America had the experience of seeing Church leaders support the powers of oppression or act in unwritten alliance with such powers. Our simple people have been accustomed to seeing the Cross blessing the oppressor's sword.

(2) In our countries conditions have never really existed in which the poor can be genuinely represented in power structures through democratic means. This was certainly true of Nicaragua. Two facts will give an idea of the world in which we lived: (a) 51 per cent of the population was illiterate and many of those who knew how to read never did so; (b) for more than fifty years, two members of the Somoza family held the reins of power.

Furthermore, the impoverishment and oppression to which the great majority were subjected meant that there were not enough candidates for public service posts after the success of the revolution.

(3) My third starting-point is that revolutionary movements that fight for justice in these countries are branded as 'terrorists' or 'subversives' by the propaganda of more powerful countries in this part of the world while the struggle is still going on, and if they are successful, this same propaganda presents them as having gone over to totalitarianism and militant atheism.

For all these reasons, I would ask that the universal Church, when thinking about the commitment made by priests in Third World countries in the political sphere, particularly in those countries where Catholicism is the majority religion, should respect the missionary principle of inculturation and not treat each case in the same way, as though it were dealing with developed countries. It should try to work out the new forms of witness that might be needed if a genuine 'option for the poor' is to be made.

1. THE PART PLAYED BY CATHOLIC PRIESTS IN THE STRUGGLE TO OVERTHROW THE DICTATORSHIP

For four centuries, our people have lived in the midst of poverty, malnutrition, illiteracy and abandonment; working in unjust and inhuman conditions, without means of communication, without health centres, without schools, without culture, with no participation in the destiny of the country, without the slightest chance of becoming the protagonists of their own history. Added to these evils, the Somoza dictatorship lasting half a century filled the country with the most appalling injustices, not only lack of liberty, but a constant and ferocious process of repression.

Our people have always been struggling, but this began to take a more organised form with the establishment of the Sandinista National Liberation Front (FSLN) in 1961. Throughout these years since the setting-up of the dictatorship, thousands of Nicaraguans had been assassinated, but new heroes always appeared to take their place, not afraid to offer the last drop of their blood to rescue their people from slavery, without fear of the Pharaoh.

Our Church lived tranquilly at peace with the oppressors. A few significant facts: (a) it is never forgotten in Nicaragua that during the funeral service for General Somoza García, the founder of the dynasty, the then Archbishop of Managua applied the title 'prince of the Church' to the dictator. (b) I shall never forget that on my return to Nicaragua in 1968, when I had been ordained priest and the struggle of the people and the repression by the authorities were growing daily, I heard my first pastoral letter from the bishops of Nicaragua. It gave no theological indication of how better to discern God's will in those difficult times; it just required that priests should all wear a black soutane. Not a word about the black situation of the country. (c) With some glorious exceptions, our Church maintained an alliance with the dictatorship. In 1968, several leaders of the FSLN were captured and then killed; on this occasion, the auxiliary Bishop of Managua wrote an article in the government paper in which he virtually justified the repression on the grounds that, in his view, these young men were communists.

I then had to leave the country for nine months, to complete my religious training with the last course we Jesuits do, called Third Probation. I asked to do this in the city of Medellín, in Colombia, since there the course had been moved from a beautiful four-storey building set in gardens and sports grounds to a shanty-town suburb in the poverty belt surrounding the city of Medellín. The year before, the Second General Conference of Latin American Bishops had been held in the city. I spent these months surrounded by people beset by hunger, unemployment and disease, without electric light, with none of the services usually provided by a town. I came to love these people deeply, and living among them marked my life for ever.

My Christian faith, my human feelings, everything I saw and heard, led me day by day to a conclusion that sprang from the depths of my being: this cannot go on like this! It is not right that there should be such suffering; God cannot be neutral in such a situation!

My spiritual experience among those poor people confirmed the impression I had received from studying the Bible: that God is not neutral, that he is a God who listens to the cry of the oppressed and takes their part. The Bible had never seemed so clear as it did reading it amidst the squalor and destitution of that shanty-town. In mid-1970 I finished my course and went back to my own country, first swearing an oath to the inhabitants of that part of Medellín: 'I will devote my life to the integral liberation of the poor of Latin America, wherever I can most usefully do so.'

I began work at the Central American University of Managua, as Vice-Rector, in charge of the students. A long dark night was covering our people: dictatorship, dependency, imprisonment, torture, hunger, corruption, malnutrition, fear, death, violation of all the most basic human and civil rights. The official Catholic Church continued to live peacefully with that genocidal regime. There were perhaps half a dozen priests who tried to put into practice the pastoral principles deriving from the Medellín documents. The FSLN was by now known to everyone and gaining the respect and sympathy of the people for its brave, clean fight against the dictatorship on behalf of the people.

Inspired by the Medellín doctrine and seeking the integral liberation of the people, some of us priests began to take part in all the civic struggles of the people for their liberation: demonstrations, occupations of churches, hunger strikes, open-air meetings, articles in the press, etc. Christian student groups also began to take part in the struggle at this time, and they were to play a very important part later. The most significant moment for Christian participation in the people's struggle was the first occupation of the Cathedral. Three priests, myself included, accompanied about a hundred students from the Catholic University in a hunger strike in Managua Cathedral in 1970, demanding respect for the lives of those university students who had been arrested in the past few days, demanding to be able to talk to them, and that, as the law of Nicaragua required, after ten days they should either be set free or taken before a magistrate with specific charges laid against them.

It was usual in Nicaragua for anyone arrested to spend weeks being tortured in the offices of National Security. The occupation of the Cathedral caused a commotion throughout the country. The army surrounded the building; we rang the bells for the dead every fifteen minutes, day and night, and declared that we would go on ringing them till justice was done and the law carried out. Large groups of people came from all the major parishes in Managua to sit in the square as a gesture of support for us, carrying banners and singing religious and protest songs. Thousands of people came, and thousands more waved to us from passing buses and cars. In three and a half days, we made the dictator give way. For the first time, a Christian group had taken part in a resounding public manifestation. Supportive documents were published by the *Cursillos de Cristiandad*, the Christian Family Movement, the Base Communities and other groups. A few days later, the Bishops' Conference of Nicaragua issued a pastoral letter condemning the occupation. Thousands of Christians signed a letter respectfully pointing out to the bishops that rather than the temple of stone, the bodies of the students were temples of the Holy Spirit, being tortured in prison. But the most basic part of this document was that which told the bishops that the people of Nicaragua had chosen their way: that of the struggle for justice, and that they, their pastors, instead of placing themselves at the head of their people, had stood aside and condemned their course. From this moment on, there was always a Christian presence in all parts of the people's struggle.

Whenever I spoke to Christian groups, I told them: Latin America is on the way to its transformation. The revolution in Nicaragua will happen soon. You must bear in mind that this revolution will happen with the Christians, without them, despite them, or against them. Years later, people in all parts of the country have reminded me of what I said then.

I knew it was important for the Church not to disqualify itself, so that young people could see that it had a care to bring justice to the exploited: paradoxically, the problem of union between Christians and revolutionaries in Nicaragua did not come from the latter, but from the Christian side. I was personally acquainted with the founder of the

FSLN, Commander-in-Chief Carlos Fonseca Amador (murdered in 1976) and I knew his open-mindedness and desire to unite with the Christians. I studied the statutes of the FSLN which he had written in 1969 and in which he spoke of religious freedom and support for those priests who worked for the people. In 1970 I met Commandant Oscar Turcios, member of the National Command of the FSLN (assassinated in 1973). He told me: 'What matters is not that you believe there is another life and that I believe I end here, but that the basic question is whether we both believe that we can work together to build a new society.'

Christian communities, particularly youth groups, began to play an increasing part in the people's slow and dangerous march to their liberation. Faith inspired thousands of Nicaraguans to commit themselves spontaneously and naturally to this struggle. They understood that fighting for justice and the poor was supporting God's cause.

When Commandant Eduardo Contreras (murdered in 1976) asked me to work for the FSLN, I could only think of the parable of the Good Samaritan, and it seemed obvious to me that I should not be like that priest and that Levite who passed by abandoning the wounded man. The Samaritans of Nicaragua were asking me to help heal our wounded people and my Christian faith gave me only one answer: engagement.

I continued working with students, giving courses of spiritual exercises, directing *Cursillos* and keeping my chair of philosophy at the Autonomous University of Nicaragua, but at the same time collaborating with the FSLN in their struggle for national liberation.

Our comradeship with the people meant bringing them our real prestige as priests, our moral demands, our struggle to preserve unity, the seed of the new man we could sow, while giving our support to the only actual force that was genuinely working to achieve justice for the people. In this, love for one's neighbour and the 'preferential option' for the poor became a reality. It was not that there were several projects compatible with the Christian ideal. This was the only one that had the possibility of enabling the people to grasp their right to participate in building their own history.

We had to show up the alliance, which till then had held between most of the official Church and the oppressive power. for the wrong it was. My studies had prepared me to be a university professor, to conduct spiritual exercises and administer the sacraments. The cry of the oppressed and the real state of my country were leading me to discover other aspects of the same priestly ministry. There was no rupture with my priesthood; I was just laying greater emphasis on the prophetic aspect of my calling. The choice was consistent with the various dimensions of the priesthood, and it made plain to me, not so much the elements of ministry known in the Old Testament, as the prophetic elements which Jesus showed in the New.

My work was becoming increasingly dangerous day by day, since most of what I did was in public. The Somoza authorities expelled me from the university. I took an active part in setting up the Christian Revolutionary Movement, which was to train a large number of cadres and leaders for the FSLN. The revolutionary leaders sent me to Washington in 1976, to denounce the crimes and violations of human rights by the Somoza dictatorship to the United States Congress. On my return to the country, the President of the Senate Chamber of Nicaragua asked that I should be declared a traitor to the country.

Among many other tasks, I founded the Nicaraguan Commission for Human Rights and organised more than a hundred day courses, retreats, conferences, etc., aimed at 'conscientising' the young people all over the country. In secret, together with other priests who were also working for the revolution, I carried out all the tasks the FSLN assigned to me.

In October 1977, the government would not let me leave the country, so I escaped over the mountains in order to go to San José in Costa Rica to join those selected by the

FSLN to form the so-called 'Group of Twelve', as a political front of the guerrilla struggle. There are a thousand other incidents connected with our hopes, struggles and fears in those days which I cannot set down here for lack of space. Motivated always by faith, but often walking in the dark, trying to see and follow the Lord of history, when all we could see was crime and the smiling dictator emerging victorious from every incident. . . . Hope was sometimes darkened. I was often afraid, very much afraid, especially of being tortured.

Despite the order out to arrest us, we returned to Nicaragua on 4 July 1978, but had to go underground in less than two months. Then came the uprising in September and the final offensive in the following year, when, after the heroic sacrifice of 50,000 compatriots who gave their lives in the final fifty-two days of fighting, we achieved the people's victory on 19 July 1979.

We were not the only priests doing something for the struggle; many others supported us in their preaching of the gospel, and many, many religious, men and women, collaborated with the guerrillas in all sorts of ways, while thousands of Christians fought in all the trenches and at all the barricades of the fields and the cities of Nicaragua.

When the final triumph of our people came, I had been actively engaged in working for their liberation for more than ten years. At no time during this period were my decisions motivated by any sort of crisis in my vocation; for me it was simply the progress of a priest who came into contact with the prophetic dimension of his priesthood and the demands this made in a country like ours.

I should add that every step I took in those ten years was taken in consultation with and with the approval of my religious superiors and my religious community.

2. AFTER THE VICTORY

Once the revolution had triumphed, I could have retired from political activism. I did not do so because I saw that there was still a long struggle ahead. Our organisation was weak, tremendously beset by powerful forces; continuing to support it did not mean taking a share in some power structure, but increasing the possibility of the poor gaining power. Also, I was determined to pursue the project of forming the new man in the new structure, keeping up the presence of Christian values in it, and maintaining the possibility that for the first time, a Leftist party *in power* should not be anti-Christian. And this historic possibility was threatened and weak.

So I offered what I had: experience in international relations through a missionary background and a role in administering a large missionary congregation; languages, contacts, etc.; experience in the cultural field, having worked to link learned and popular culture; experience in the field of education of young people and taking part in their organisations; experience in social work through my parish responsibilities.

I felt that the eyes of Latin America were upon me, that I symbolised a break with the power structures of the Church. I could not let my colleagues down. And what I have reaped from political office has been hard work, sacrifice, threats of assassination and kidnapping, none of the privilege usually associated with it.

What I have also found is that the tasks entrusted to me have been wholly consonant with those appropriate to my priestly calling. Fifteen days after the victory of the revolution, its leaders appointed me National Co-ordinator of the National Literacy Crusade. The whole people was involved in this effort, and most of our students went off to the countryside to teach, succeeding in reducing the incidence of illiteracy from 51 per cent to 12·9 per cent in five months of all-out effort. It was our second uprising. I felt more fulfilled as a priest teaching our people to read than teaching Plato and Aristotle at the university. Every week-end I went out to the fields and the hills, seeing how this great work of love was progressing, how brotherhood between students and peasants was growing.

Never had a task required so much work and dedication from me. There had been eight months of preparing the project, followed by five months of the campaign itself. I practically lived in my office—I didn't move my bed in there only because there was no room for it! And calls kept coming to me at home during the night: emergencies arising—including fifty-nine students killed or wounded because they were teaching our people to read, of whom seven were murdered by counter-revolutionary forces. These thousands of young people teaching the country to read were the 'new man' who had made his appearance in Nicaragua.

The Christian contribution to this epic task was a major one. At the Closing Session of the Second Literacy Congress, Comrade Carlos Carrión Cruz, the FSLN Directorate delegate to the Literary Crusade, said of it: 'We must also point out that there are tons of ink and paper being used in trying to convince Christians that they cannot be Christians and revolutionaries at the same time. But the true Christians, religious and lay, have not wasted their time on these theoretical debates. Through their outstanding participation in the Crusade, they have shown in practical terms that not only is it possible to be a Christian and a revolutionary, but that if one is a Christian one also has to be a revolutionary.'

After the Literacy Crusade had been completed, the FSLN agreed to my request to work with the '19 July Sandinista Youth' movement and appointed me a member of its National Executive Committee. I know the work I am now doing there can easily be censured by the official Church as 'political work', but the important thing is that the Sandinista revolution has placed a priest in charge of the formation of the most precious asset it possesses: its young people, and so its future. As a priest and as a teacher, I have felt deeply fulfilled through working with an organisation involving more than 60 per cent of the students of Nicaragua.

The Sandinista leaders also entrusted the Ministry of Culture to Fr Ernesto Cardenal, the Ministry of Foreign Affairs to another priest, Fr Miguel D'Escoto, and the Ministry of Social Welfare to yet another, Fr Edgard Parrales. They are the visible signs of one of the basic realities of the Sandinista revolution: the Christian presence throughout its whole process.

CONCLUSION

We are conscious of being exceptional or 'frontier' cases in the practice legally allowed by the Church. We do not claim that our case should be generalised, nor do we expect all the revolutions gathering momentum in Latin America to appoint priests to ministerial posts in the government they form. The permission we received from the Bishops' Conference in June 1981 to stay in our posts was based on the consideration that this was 'an exception in the emergency' in which we Nicaraguans still find ourselves after the war of liberation.

But through being on the frontier, we do consider that we are carrying out an apostolic mission entirely proper to the priesthood, exercising a role of leadership, a service in faith in the midst of a secular historical movement. which we claim to be helping not merely not to become anti-religious, or anti Christian, but to be truly 'revolutionary', human in the revolution, a true servant of the poor.

I would say that what is at stake is not a canon of Church law, but that faith should really open itself to the possibility of being incarnate in the option for the poor, and that all over the world it should expect to break its links with the ruling powers.

The importance for the future of a nation that the leaders of its revolution should publicly recognise the part played by Christians in it can hardly be overestimated. The official communiqué on religion issued by the National Leadership of the FSLN on 7 October 1980, contains sentences such as these: 'Christian patriots and revolutionaries are an integral part of the Sandinista Popular Revolution, and have been for many years . . .'; 'A large number of the militants and combatants of the FSLN found the motivation for joining the revolutionary struggle and therefore the FSLN in their interpretation of their faith . . .'; 'These were all humble men who were prepared to carry out their patriotic and revolutionary duties without becoming involved in long philosophical discussions . . .'; 'Christians have been an integral part of our revolutionary history to a degree unprecedented in any other revolutionary movement in Latin America, and possibly in the world.'

I believe that we in Nicaragua should be allowed to say something about Jesus Christ through our actions, through our witness, encouraging and accompanying those Christians who are living within a historical process, which in itself also tells and teaches us something of the spirit of Jesus.

Translated by Paul Burns

David van Ooijen

Priests in Politics

1. INTRODUCTION

FROM THE end of the nineteenth century, in 1880, until the present day, priests have always formed part of the Dutch parliament. Protestant clergymen entered parliament even before that date. This participation of members of the Catholic and Protestant clergy in the government was accepted by the Dutch people in the conviction that every citizen, whatever his status, profession, race or position in society, could be elected to represent the people of the Netherlands. It is true, of course, that, according to the Constitutional Law of 1848 to 1887, the function of a people's representative could not be exercised by members of the clergy 'for as long as they were invested with the dignity of their pastoral office'. In practice, however, this meant that Roman Catholic priests had to resign from their posts as parish priests or as professors in seminaries. It was not regarded as an obstacle in the eyes of the law that a priest was, in that case, still competent to function as a priest.

There was also little opposition on the part of the Church province to priests entering parliament. The permission of the bishop—or the superior in the case of a religious—was required according to canon law, but this was normally granted. What is more, at least until 1981, the ordinary never publicly criticised a priest who was a member of parliament for his political standpoint and pronouncements.

There was also no official criticism from Rome that priests had seats in the Dutch parliament. Dr H. J. A. M. Schaepman and Dr W. H. Nolens, both of whom were members of parliament, the first for twenty-three years and the second for thirty-five years, were even appointed by the Holy See as domestic prelates, in recognition of their political activities. In 1923, when he became Minister of State in the Dutch government, Nolens was also made an apostolic protonotary by the Holy See.

Up till now, ten Roman Catholic priests have been members of the Dutch parliament. Some of them have been diocesan priests and others have been members of religious orders. In most cases, their political activities ceased when they died or were not re-elected. In one case only, a priest had to cease being politically active because of intervention on the part of the Church authorities. That happened in 1981.

2. THE CATHOLIC PARTY

One special aspect of the situation in the Netherlands has been that, from 1880

76

onwards, Roman Catholic priests have been active in politics both as people's representatives and as leaders of the Catholic part of the population. Of fundamental importance in the rise of the Catholic Party in the Netherlands was desire felt by Dutch Catholics for emancipation and equal rights. I have already mentioned Dr Schaepman. He was born in 1844 and died in 1903. He was a priest in the diocese of Utrecht and was virtually the founder of the Catholic Party. He was also its leader for many years in the Lower Chamber, being succeeded by another priest, Dr Nolens (1860-1931), of the diocese of Roermond. Nolens was the leader of the largest party represented in the government for very many years and had a very important influence on the conduct of affairs in the country. It was during his period of political leadership that the Protestants, who had previously opposed equal rights for the Catholic section of the population, became less and less strongly opposed to the Catholic Party. The new opponents were, in the opinion of the Catholic members, the socialists and the liberals. It is interesting to note that, in 1883, Schaepman denied that Catholics 'who did not want to be counted as members of this party had lost the right to be called Catholic',[1] while, in 1924, Nolens declared, with reference to the Catholic Party, that 'every Catholic voter finds his rightful place in it and not in any other party'.[2]

This statement was entirely in accordance with the view of the Dutch bishops. As early as 1906, they had written that 'it is their earnest and emphatic desire that the Catholics who are subject to them should be united and kept united in Catholic organisations'. In this, the bishops were convinced that they were acting in accordance with what Pope Pius X had written in his letter to the Italian Christian Democrats. In 1910, the same pope reiterated the same views in a rather more emphatic way in his letter condemning the French interconfessional organisation *Sillon*. In this letter, he said: 'The leaders of *Sillon* believed that they had a right to think and act independently of the hierarchy, because they thought that their concerns were of a purely temporal nature. In fact, however, there was, underlying their programme, a morality, on the basis of which the leaders of *Sillon* believed that the movement was Christian and Catholic. Since they were thus clearly entering the religious sphere, the clergy had also to be represented and given a voice in the movement. The rejection of this claim made by the clergy was a gross attack against the Church itself.'[3]

Children of Catholic families were at a very early age confronted with the close bond that the Church leaders wished to maintain between the Church and the political attitude of its members. A typical example is this sentence taken from a junior school reader that was used in the 1930s: 'A good Catholic votes for a Catholic candidate.'[4] During elections, even sharper pronouncements were made. According to the chairman of the Catholic Party in 1922, for example, 'Even the slightest deviation from Catholic policy may lead to a person dying outside the Holy Church and not being given a Catholic burial'.[5]

It is hardly surprising that an important part has been played in the Catholic Party in the Netherlands by priests. After all, the Catholic Church and the Catholic Party were for a long time identified with each other and the latter was seen as 'a direct result of the unity that dominates the entire economy by virtue of our Roman Catholic teaching about faith and morals'.[6] Many priests, including especially Ariëns and Poels, did not exercise political functions directly, but they certainly exercised a very powerful political influence. After the Second World War, the Protestant parties declined and there were many serious economic problems in the country. This meant that the Catholic Party was no longer able to obtain a sufficient majority to form a government without the support of the socialists and/or the liberals. In this situation, priests continued to carry out important functions in the Catholic Party. Because of their collaboration with the Catholic Party, however, the socialists and liberals could no longer be described as those 'whose fundamental principles were diametrically opposed to Catholic principles' (Nolens)[7] and it consequently became less and less automatic for Catholics to vote for the Catholic Party. More and more Catholics voted for, supported and even joined both the socialists and the liberals.

This was regarded with disfavour both by the Catholic Party and by the Catholic bishops. In their declaration of 1954, the latter said that membership of a political party other than the Catholic Party was 'not the way to build up society in the Christian spirit' and that 'following that way could not be justified'.[8] But the bishops' call to unity among Catholics in the political sphere by supporting the Catholic Party as in the past fell on many deaf ears. A considerable number of Catholics refused to conform to the wishes of their bishops because they felt that they could not in conscience do it.

The opinion was expressed with increasing frequency in the 1960s, when the Catholic Party, as the parliamentary representative of Catholic associations and institutions, was very rapidly becoming less automatically accepted, that it was in fact outdated. The situation changed in the 1970s, when the Catholic Party functioned in close co-operation with the two Protestant parties. Finally, since the 1981 elections in the Netherlands, these parties have joined together definitively to form a single new party, the so-called Christian Democratic Appèl (Appeal). The Catholic Party has ceased to exist as such.

The participation of priests and others holding office in the churches in politics is now almost universally accepted in the Netherlands. Possibly because they have not wanted to be outdone by the Catholic Party, other parties have for some time now also accepted priests and ministers as parliamentary candidates and members. Again, possibly because the Catholic Party did not want to appear to be clinging to a monopoly, little resistance was offered by its members to this tendency. Indeed, it is true to say that it has often been seen as evidence of complete emancipation that every citizen of the Netherlands—and that, of course, means every priest or minister of religion—could be appointed to any office.

3. THE ATTITUDE OF THE CHURCH AUTHORITIES

As I have already indicated, the Church authorities in the Netherlands have on the whole placed few obstacles in the way of priests who have wanted to enter parliament. All ten priests who have so far been members of the Dutch parliament have obtained the permission from their ordinary that is required by canon law.[9] As far as we know, the bishops have also never, at least until recently, publicly criticised priests in parliament for the way in which they have voted, expressed themselves or carried out their functions.

Bearing in mind the prevalent attitudes at each period, there has often been quite good reason for them to express criticism. At the beginning of this century, for example, Schaepman was the only Catholic member of parliament to vote for the introduction of compulsory education, with the result that this Bill became law with the smallest possible majority. Schaepman also spoke strongly in favour of compulsory military service and universal suffrage, at a time when many Catholics regarded these two questions as directly contradicting the law of God.

It was not until a hundred years after Dr Schaepman's entry into parliamentary affairs as the first priest member of the Upper House that open conflict occurred in this sphere. In 1981, Dr J. Gijsen, the Bishop of Roermond, made it clear to one of his priests, M. G. G. J. Schreurs, that he should give up his seat in the Upper Chamber or Senate as a member of the Christian Democratic Appèl because he had voted for the proposition made by the government to liberalise the legislation concerning induced abortion. Partly because of Schreurs' vote, this proposition was accepted with a very small majority. I should perhaps mention in this context that I myself abstained from voting for this Bill simply because I thought that the degree of liberalisation was insufficient and therefore hardly possible to put into practice.

In addition to criticising Schreurs for voting for this Bill, Bishop Gijsen also told him in his letter that 'the pope had made it even more obvious recently than in the past that he did not like to see parliamentary activity being performed by a priest'.

In view of the fact that this priest had accepted membership of the Upper Chamber after having obtained explicit consent from the Conference of Dutch Bishops, he naturally enough asked the other bishops to intervene in his case. As a direct result of this appeal, Cardinal J. Willebrands, the Archbishop of Utrecht, made this declaration: 'The Catholic members of the Upper and Lower Houses do not represent the Church, but the people who have elected them. They are, of course, both as people and as politicians, bound to certain principles of faith and ethics. Every person, whether he is a Christian or not, has certain ethical insights and principles which to some extent determine his judgment and his actions. The politician is confronted with the question as to how he can validate these principles in the government and the legislature of his country. He is personally responsible and has to make a personal judgment in this question. He should not deviate from his principles, but he has to know the concrete situation and look for possible ways in which he can express those principles for the well-being of his country. In his political and parliamentary activity he is personally responsible and must act according to his own conscience with regard to those who have elected him and before God.'[10]

Cardinal Willebrands' reaction, which was made public in the name of the other bishops, was widely interpreted as an indication that the Dutch bishops did not want to associate themselves with the Bishop of Roermond in this instance. Dr Gijsen, however, stuck to his guns and refused to grant the permission that the Code of Canon Law required to his priest to take up his seat. He even threatened to suspend the priest if he in fact took up the seat. There seemed to be little prospect of success in an appeal to Rome, since canon law defined that a priest had a duty to obtain consent, but it did not hold out any prospect of a right. We are, however, justified in concluding that the great majority of bishops and religious superiors in the Netherlands regard it as acceptable, subject to certain conditions, that priests should be active in politics.

This is not necessarily the case in other countries.[11] I was, for example, asked personally by the Bishop of Münster (the Federal Republic of West Germany) 'to cease taking part in political gatherings in West Germany', after I had appeared at a forum there as a member of the Council of Europe. This is in striking contrast to the fact that the German bishops normally express their views about concrete political questions in public before elections in such a way that their preference for the Christian Democrats emerges quite clearly. At the same time, it seems to have escaped their notice that priests in West Germany often strongly urge their congregations to vote for the Christian Democrats in their sermons. In the Netherlands, too, it sometimes happens that priests use the pulpit to express a preference for a certain political party, although this preference is not exclusively for the Christian Democrats. It is, however, true to say that in the vast majority of cases the pulpit is not used as a platform by priests to influence their congregations in their choice of candidates. In view of the fact that Catholics in the Netherlands are in the custom of making a free political choice, any attempt on the part of their priests to urge them to vote for one party or another would not go unchallenged.

4. THE PAPAL NUNCIO

Until quite recently, the papal nuncio in the Netherlands was in regular contact with

Catholic politicians, but only with those who belonged to the Catholic or the Christian Democratic Parties and not at all with Catholic members of other parliamentary parties. More recently, this formal contact ceased to exist. I am not able to judge whether it has continued in an informal way or not.

Over the ten years that I have served in parliament, I have personally never experienced any attempt on the part of the nuncio or his staff to influence my own political attitude or point of view. It has certainly happened that Catholic ministers have been approached by the nuncio as members of the Roman Catholic Church and it is quite clear in these cases that decisions were expected of them that they had to take as Catholic ministers. Ministers in the Dutch government are traditionally expected to justify their decisions in great detail in parliament and Catholics are in a minority in that assembly. In view of this, it can reasonably be assumed that any attempts made by the nuncio to persuade Catholic ministers to account for their decisions precisely as Catholics can hardly ever have led to a concrete result in their attitude as ministers.

5. WHY SHOULD PRIESTS BE MEMBERS OF PARLIAMENT?

The situation in the Netherlands, which is characterised by the fact that priests have for many years been active members of the Catholic Party, provided me with a very good reason for engaging in politics. I entered the political arena precisely because I did not feel drawn in any way to the Catholic Party. That party was acceptable to a considerable number of Catholics partly because many priests supported it and even accepted functions in it. I, on the other hand, did not take it for granted in any way that the Catholic Party necessarily had the most acceptable policy from the Christian point of view. From 1901 onwards, it had been represented almost without interruption in the government of the country. The policy of Catholics generally and that of the Catholic Party had been so closely identified for so long that the few Catholics who voted for other parties were often regarded as less Catholic. This had led to many Catholics, and especially those who tended to be left-wing, becoming alienated from the Church.

My decision to make myself available as a representative of the people was therefore at least partly based on a feeling of solidarity with those Dutch Catholics who had, in my opinion, been disqualified, as it were, by the negative judgment that their bishops had pronounced at various times, but especially in 1954, concerning their personal political choice. This was in any case how quite a number of those Catholics saw my political career from the very beginning. This was one reason why I entered politics, but not as a 'Catholic' member. There was, however, also a much more profound reason.

My deeper reason for becoming a politician was my conviction that the Church also has a political task that must be carried out not only by lay people, but also by priests as those who lead the Christian community. In my view, this political task has to be expressed, among other things, in resisting the arms race and all attempts to perfect the nuclear weapons that are capable of destroying the world.

Translated by David Smith

Notes

1. H. J. A. M. Schaepman *Een katholieke partij. Proeve van een program* (Utrecht 1883).
2. W. H. Nolens Debates in the Lower House (1924) during the period preceding the budget of 1925.

3. *AAS* II (1909) 611.

4. This quotation is taken from a reader used in the older classes of Roman Catholic primary schools in the 1930s: *Mensch en Maatschappij* ('s-Hertogenbosch 1933).

5. P. J. Oud *Het Jongste Verleden. Parlementaire geschiedenis van Nederland* (Assen 1948) II p. 42.

6. B. Kruitwagen *Verslagboek van de Tweede Katholiekendag* p. 204.

7. J. Colsen 'Poels' (Roermond and Maaseik 1955) p. 68.

8. Pronouncement of the Dutch bishops (1954) p. 43.

9. The ten priests who have served in the Dutch parliament are: Mgr Dr H. J. A. M. Schaepman (1844-1903), member of the Lower House from 1880 to 1903, Catholic Party; Mgr Dr W. Everts (1827-1900), member of the Lower House from 1893 to 1984, Catholic Party; Mgr Dr W. H. Nolens (1860-1931), member of the Lower House from 1896 to 1931, Catholic Party; Dr L. J. C. Beaufort, OFM (1890-1965), member of the Lower House from 1937 to 1946 and of the Upper House from 1948 to 1963, Catholic Party; Dr J. C. Stokman, OFM (1903-1970), member of the Lower House from 1946 to 1967 and of the Upper House from 1967 to 1969, Catholic Party; J. A. Heijmans (1923-1974), member of the Lower House from 1971 to 1974, Catholic Party; Dr A. J. Agterberg, OESA (1925-1977), member of the Lower House from 1973 to 1977, Radical Party; M. W. M. van Winkel, OSB, member of the Lower House from 1975 to 1977, Radical Party; Dr M. G. G. J. Schreurs, member of the Lower House from 1980 to 1981, Christian Democratic Appèl; Dr D. A. T. van Ooijen OP, member of the Lower House from 1971 to the present, Socialist Partij van de Arbeid.

10. Information bulletin of the Secretariat of the Roman Catholic Province of the Church in the Netherlands, Year 9, No. 10, 22 June 1981, p. 251.

11. As an example of the difference in other countries, see the report in the Belgian daily paper *De Standaard*, 29 June 1981, on the *IJzerbedevaart* or 'Iron Pilgrimage', a demonstration made by Flemish-speaking Belgians against their French-speaking compatriots: 'The crowd, dressed in raincoats, discreetly listened to the celebration of the Eucharist. Following the theme of the pilgrimage, the Mass was entrusted to priests from the threatened territories—the Voer, Komen, Brussels and the marginal communities.' It is clearly also possible to be active politically as a priest without openly admitting it—through the ministry of the sacraments!

George Higgins

A Common Law Country (USA)

CURRENT CHURCH law on the involvement of clerics in elected political office is found in the Code of Canon Law, primarily in Canon 139, paragraphs 1, 2, and 4. Rosemary Smith, SC, a doctoral candidate in canon law at the Catholic University of America, has carefully analysed this canon as interpreted in 1922 by the Code Commission, in 1927 and 1957 by the Sacred Congregation of the Council, and in 1966 by Pope Paul VI in his *Motu Proprio De Episcoporum Muneribus*. Smith concludes this section of her study paper as follows: 'The cumulative effect of the wording of Canon 139 and the subsequent interpretation of it is that the official Church views clergy in elected political office quite negatively and that it is ready to back this position up with serious sanctions.'[1]

Vatican Council II and the 1971 Synod of Bishops, while stressing a more open and more missionary view of the role of the Church (and the role of the clergy) in relation to the world, basically maintained the 1917 Code's sharp distinction between priestly ministry and secular activities, between activities which properly belong to the clergy and those which properly belong to lay people. The 1971 Synod left an opening, however, for the involvement of the clergy in elected political office under exceptional circumstances, subject to the consent of the local ordinary after consultation with the priests' council and, if necessary, with the national or regional episcopal conferences. But since the Synod of Bishops, as presently constituted, is only an advisory body, no specific legislation resulted from the 1971 gathering on the subject under discussion here. Its final document on The Ministerial Priesthood simply expressed the mind of the Synod in the light of which all subsequent legislation should be shaped. In Smith's judgment, the proposed new legislation, as outlined in the Schema *De Populo Dei*, is even more specific and consequently more restrictive than the present legislation. I share Smith's opinion that this proposed legislation is too inflexible and too restrictive. 'It would seem', she concludes, 'that new legislation should be much broader, with provision for particular law to be determined by the various episcopal conferences. Such an approach might better enable the Church to protect the dignity and purpose of those in ordained ministry and its own political independence while at the same time incorporating the best of the political tradition of the country and providing for a valid, if exceptional, ministry.'[2]

For the limited purposes of this paper, however, the canonical aspects of the subject under discussion can be put to one side. We will not be expected to critique present or prospective Church legislation on this subject or the theology on which it is based.

Suffice it to say that this theology, with its rigid separation of the clerical state from the lay state, needs to be refined and updated. I say this as one who, in the practical order (at least so far as the United States is concerned) is not greatly perturbed by the Church's discipline on this matter. That is to say, I see no pressing need, at least in the United States, for the involvement of the clergy in elected political office and, other things being equal, would generally advise against it.

Whatever of that, there is not likely to be any significant change in the Church's discipline on this matter within the foreseeable future. It is clear that Pope John Paul II is strongly committed to the present discipline, that, if anything, he will strengthen it and can be expected to enforce it even more strictly than his immediate predecessors. In fact, he has already done so rather dramatically in a celebrated case involving Fr Robert F. Drinan, SJ, who, in May 1980, was ordered by Rome not to stand for re-election as a member of the US House of Representatives. This paper will briefly analyse the Drinan affair, but not in theological or canonical terms. It will be a brief commentary on the procedures followed by Rome in this particular case—a case which, from the practical point of view, was, in this writer's judgment, rather badly handled.

The basic facts in the Drinan case can be summarised briefly as follows:

Fr Drinan, former Dean of the prestigious School of Law at Boston College, a Jesuit institution, was first elected to the US House of Representatives in 1970 and served for five terms, or a total of ten years. On 27 April 1980, Fr Edward M. O'Flaherty, SJ, Provincial of the New England Jesuit Province and Drinan's religious superior, received a telephone call from the Rome headquarters of the Jesuit Order directing Drinan not to run for re-election. The directive was issued by Fr Pedro Arrupe, Superior General of the Society of Jesus. Fr Arrupe said later that he was acting on the Drinan case 'at the express wish' of Pope John Paul II.

O'Flaherty, as he later reported to the press, immediately communicated the Arrupe directive to Drinan and then for the next few days pursued several avenues of appeal, stressing with the Roman authorities the fact that such an order would almost certainly seem in the eyes of many people to be an improper intrusion by the Church into American political affairs. He also pointed out the serious inconvenience to the election process itself since the filing deadline for candidates was 6 May. On 3 May, O'Flaherty was informed that his concerns about the Arrupe directive had been personally conveyed to the Vatican authorities, but that after further discussion it became clear that the decision would be final. That afternoon O'Flaherty met with Drinan in Boston. Convinced that the decision was final, Drinan agreed to announce his withdrawal from the election campaign. In a statement issued to the press that day, O'Flaherty noted that an exception had been made for Drinan when he first ran for Congress in 1970. That exception had been upheld by various Jesuit Provincials in succeeding years, he said.

'Nevertheless,' O'Flaherty continued, 'it is obvious that, in the pope's view, the reasons that commended the idea of Fr Drinan's candidacy up to now no longer apply. . . . That Pope John Paul II was moving towards such a view of things had been signalled more than once since his election to the papacy in October 1978.'

O'Flaherty assured the press that Drinan was not being singled out by the pope or by Fr Arrupe for his political activity. 'It has been stressed to me', he said, 'that Vatican and Jesuit authorities in Rome wish to underline the point that the principal reason for the order was the pope's convictions about the proper role of the priest. Indeed, one highly-placed Vatican official privately expressed the hope that it might be possible to persuade people that the pope was acting exclusively out of principle.'

Commenting on the Drinan case, several Church officials in Boston, Washington, and Rome stressed that the order directing Drinan not to run for re-election was not a new discipline initiated by the pope, but was a reaffirmation of existing Church discipline.

It was not entirely clear what effect the order relating to Drinan might have on other priests involved in elected political posts in the United States and elsewhere in the world. But at least one other US priest saw it affecting him. The day after Fr Drinan announced his decision, Fr Robert J. Cornell, OPraem of DePere, Wisconsin, said that he would not continue with his own plans to seek the Congressional seat which he had lost two years previously. Fr Cornell had served with Drinan in Congress during the mid-1970s and was hoping to return there in January 1981. Cornell first heard of the Drinan directive on 4 May. He got the news initially through calls from the media for his response to the Drinan case. Cornell decided not to run for re-election because he had been led to believe that a special papal directive forbidding priests to hold elected political office had been issued and was being transmitted through the proper channels to his religious superiors. This was a misunderstanding on his part. No such papal directive has been issued as of this writing.

In the light of this capsule-like summary of the basic facts involved in the Drinan case, I would criticise Rome's procedures on several grounds.

First of all, the precipitous and extremely awkward timing of the directive to Drinan (and secondarily to Cornell) was widely perceived as betraying almost total disregard for the practical realities of the American electoral process. William F. Buckley, Jr, an influential conservative American journalist who has long been critical of Drinan's politics and who agrees in substance with the Roman directive, put it this way in a widely-syndicated newspaper column: '. . . it would have been more prudent for the Vatican to have said that effective (let us say) in 1985, all priests serving political parties should conclude arrangements to withdraw from their official responsibilities. In that way the retreat from public life by Fr Drinan might have been done with greater aplomb. As it is, he has borne his cross with grace. . . '.

Drinan has indeed borne his cross with grace, but Rome, in my judgment, showed a lack of sensitivity in saddling him with such a heavy cross on extremely short notice and without consulting him adequately in advance. Its procedures, however well motivated, were widely perceived as being callous and heavy-handed.

Secondly, and more importantly, Rome's failure to issue even a brief and perfunctory statement outlining its own theological and pastoral rationale for the Drinan directive, was not only unfair to Drinan, but, as the record will show, was also counter-productive for Rome itself. By neglecting to make such a statement, Rome, whether wittingly or not, clearly left the impression that its directive was *ad hominem*—that is was aimed not at priest politicians in general and across the board, but at Drinan specifically (and, again, secondarily at Cornell). As indicated above, Vatican spokesmen have denied this, but the majority of Americans of all faiths who have publicly commented on the Drinan case remain incredulous.

Be that as it may, Rome's failure to provide a persuasive rationale for the Drinan directive and the selective manner in which it has chosen to enforce Church discipline on the political role of the clergy has inevitably reinforced the impression that, despite all protestations to the contrary, its directive was in fact aimed principally, if not exclusively, at Drinan. Moreover, by limiting its directive to priests holding elected political office, Rome has, in effect, given its blessing to other priests who, though not holding elected office, are deeply involved in the most partisan kind of politics. One American example will suffice. Fr Donald Shea, CPpS has, for several years, been employed as a full-time member of the staff of the national committee of the Republican Party in the United States. His one and only responsibility is to persuade Catholics to vote for that Party. Surely this is partisan politics with a vengeance. Nevertheless Fr Shea has not been told by the Vatican to resign his post and is not likely to be given any such directive in the foreseeable future. Even people sympathetic to Rome's directive in the Drinan case are perplexed by this inconsistency on Rome's part and are hard put to defend it on rational grounds.

All of this has predictably resulted in an unseemly guessing game as to who or what precipitated the Drinan directive. Many observers are convinced that influential critics of Drinan's controversial position on the abortion issue (a position with which I happen to disagree but which is too complex to be discussed adequately in this brief article) successfully pressured Rome into moving against him. Others argue—less plausibly, it would seem—that Rome, by singling out Drinan, meant to serve notice on the Society of Jesus to put its house in order and to keep its members on a short rein. Still others have suggested that Rome was using Drinan as a means for getting a message to radical or liberationist priests in Latin America and possibly in other parts of the world as well. In all fairness, Drinan should have been spared the embarrassing publicity surrounding all of this speculation.

Rome also did itself a disservice by failing to explain the Drinan directive in terms that the general public could understand. Surely there is a better case to be made for Rome's position on this matter than Rome has thus far been able or willing to make. Its failure to make that case persuasively has also led many Americans (and probably many people in other countries as well) to conclude that Rome wants priests to withdraw not only from partisan political activity but from political activity of any kind at all and is opposed to any and all forms of clerical activism, even non-political activism, in support of justice and human rights. In this regard, a respected American journalist was speaking for many other well-informed and serious-minded Americans, Catholics included, when she wrote in a widely-syndicated column that 'social activism even for justice is something the pope opposes in the clergy. . . . The ban on Drinan . . . will undoubtedly have a chilling effect on others who see themselves doing the Lord's work in public service.'

In the light of my own experience in the field of Catholic social action, I am convinced that this is a serious misreading of the intent of Rome's directive in the Drinan case, but unfortunately Rome itself is principally to blame for this confusion. Because its directive was not preceded or followed with an explanatory theological and pastoral statement, it was doomed inevitably to be misunderstood or misinterpreted even by sympathetic observers, including reasonably well-informed Catholics. For the same reason, Rome's directive will inevitably be grist to the mill of reactionaries, especially in a number of Third World countries where priests in ever-increasing numbers have joined the struggle for social justice and human rights. Reactionary forces in these countries and even in some of the economically developed nations will pre-dictably try to use the Drinan directive to silence socially-minded priests, their self-serving and deliberately misleading argument being that Rome wants priests back in the sacristy.

In summary, to quote William F. Buckley again, 'Everything about the Vatican's order issued to the Rev. Robert F. Drinan to withdraw from Congress was clumsy. Most conspicuously unfortunate was the smell of a bill of attainder. It was a single priest engaged in a discrete re-election campaign who was told to withdraw. . . . The diplomacy of the episode was inept. And the pity of it is that the pope's general position is eminently defensible.'

Buckley's frank but respectful criticism of the Drinan directive is all the more credible, as indicated earlier, because he is publicly known to be critical of Fr Drinan's particular brand of politics and also because he strongly agrees with Rome that clerics should not run for political office and, indeed, should be canonically prohibited from doing so. My own position on this matter is more nuanced than Buckley's. While, as a general rule, I can see no urgent need for priests to run for political office under partisan auspices, I would allow for exceptions (as Rome itself obviously does in practice). As indicated above, I would therefore favour a flexible approach to this problem in the new Code of Canon Law, with provision for particular law to be determined in response to local or national needs and with the widest possible consultation.

Notes

1. R. Smith *Clergy and Elected Political Office* (Department of Canon Law, School of Religious Studies, Catholic University of America, Washington, DC).
2. *ibid.*

Contributors

PIERO BELLINI was born in Bologna in 1926, and studied at the University of Rome, the Pontifical Atheneum of the Lateran and the Graduate School of Yale. He lectured in Church law and political history at Ferrara and in Church law at Pisa, and since 1974 has lectured in canon law at the University of Florence. He has published some 100 books and articles in various reviews, mainly on dogmatic and historical aspects of the Church-State relationship, including *Principi di diritto ecclesiastico* (1972-1976); *Libertà dell' nomo e fattore religioso rei sistemi ideologici contemporanei* (1975); *Chiesa e realtà politiche* (1977, 1980).

GUY VAN DEN BRANDE. Born in Lier (Belgium) in 1957, the author is a lawyer attached to the Court of Malines. He obtained his bachelor's degree in canon law, his licentiate in law and his qualification as a solicitor at the Catholic University of Louvain. At present he is completing his studies at the Institut Universitaire de Hautes Etudes Internationales in Geneva. He belonged to a society of canon lawyers and published a number of articles on the role the Catholic Church plays at international level.

FERNANDO CARDENAL MARTINEZ, SJ, was born in 1934 in Granada, Nicaragua. He studied classics and philosophy at the Catholic University of Quito, and theology at the Jesuit College in Mexico. Appointed Vice-Rector of the Central American University in Managua in 1970, he moved to the Autonomous National University of Nicaragua, where he held the chair of philosophy from 1973-1977. After the victory of the Sandinista revolution, he was appointed National Co-ordinator of the Literacy Crusade. He is now a member of the National Executive Committee for Sandinista Youth, a member of the Board of Directors of the Central American University, and a member of the Sandinista Assembly.

HELMUT GELLER was born in 1945 and has been awarded doctorates in both sociology and theology. His work has included research into the problems of inter-church married couples, carried out at the Catholic ecumenical institute in the University of Münster. He is at present a teacher.

ALBERT P. GNÄGI was born in 1944. He studied law in Zürich and at the Gregorianum in Rome, and was awarded a doctorate of the University of Zürich in 1969 for a thesis on 'The Catholic Church and Democracy'. He now practises as solicitor and barrister in Zürich, and has written a number of essays on concordat law and the legal relations between Church and State.

PATRICK GRANFIELD was born in 1930. He studied at the Pontifical Institute of St Anselm in Rome and at the Catholic University of America. Doctor of philosophy and doctor of theology, he teaches systematic theology at the Catholic University of America. Among his published works are: *Theologians at Work* (1967), *Ecclesial Cybernetics: A Study of Democracy in the Church* (1973), and *The Papacy in Transition* (1980).

JAN HEIJKE was born in Amsterdam in 1927. He studied theology at Nijmegen and Louvain, and lectured in theology from 1955 to 1970 at Gemert and Eindhoven. From 1972 to 1974 he was secretary of studies at the secretariat of the Roman Catholic Church province at Utrecht. Since 1974 he has been lecturing at the theological faculty of Nijmegen, in the missiology department. He has made various study trips to Africa: Cameroon, Tanzania (1968), Central African Republic (1970-1971), Chad (1971), People's Republic of the Congo (Brazzaville) (1977), Algeria (1980), Zaïre (1982). He is the editor of the missiological journal *Wereld en Zending*. His publications include: *The Image of God According to Saint Augustine* (De Trinitate *excepted*) (Notre Dame, Ind. 1956); *An Ecumenical Light on the Renewal of Religious Community Life: Taizé* (Pittsburgh 1967); *De bijbel over geloven* (Roermond/Maaseik 1965); 'Socialism and Church in Africa' *Exchange* (Leiden) 10 (1982) No. 30.

GEORGE G. HIGGINS was born in Chicago, Illinois, in 1916. After his seminary studies he did graduate study in economics and political science at the Catholic University of America and later at the Institute for Continuing Theological Education, Rome. Ordained a priest in 1940, elevated to Papal Chamberlain in 1953 and named a Domestic Prelate in 1959, he has taught in the Department of Economics, Catholic University, was appointed to the staff of the Social Action Department, National Catholic Welfare Conference in 1944 and finally director in 1954, and was appointed Secretary for Research of the United States Catholic Conference in 1972. He became adjunct lecturer in the School of Theology, Catholic University of America in 1980. His organisational activities have included being consultant to Vatican II, being a member of the Executive Committee of the Leadership Conference on Civil Rights and adviser to the Chairman of the US Delegation to the Belgrade Conference on Human Rights. He writes a weekly syndicated column, 'The Yardstick', and occasional book reviews and articles in *Commonweal* and *America*.

HANS-HERMANN HÜCKING was born in 1942 in Göttingen. He studied at the Dominican school in Walberberg before going on to study theology at the universities of Bochum and Münster. Since 1971 he has been teaching philosophy at the Westfalen College, Dortmund. A member of the Commission for Contacts in Eastern Europe in the German section of *Pax Christi*, he works freelance for radio and journals. He has contributed articles about the churches in eastern Europe to books.

RAYMOND LEMIEUX was born in Lévis (Quebec, Canada) in 1939. He studied history and social sciences at Laval University, sociology of knowledge at the University of Paris VII and religious sciences at the Ecole des Hautes Etudes (Social Sciences). He teaches Church history and sociology of religion at Laval University.

His recent publications include articles on the changing relations between religion and politics in industrialised society and on the sociology of religion in Quebec Province.

JEAN-MARIE MAYEUR is a professor of Contemporary History at the Université de Paris IV-Sorbonne. His most important works include *La Séparation de l'Eglise et de l'Etat* (1966); *Les Débuts de la Troisième République* (1973); *Des Partis catholiques à la démocratie chrétienne* (1980).

JOHANNES NEUMANN was professor of ecclesiastical law in the University of Tübingen, but in 1977 relinquished his ecclesiastical responsibilities. Since 1978 he has been professor of the sociology of law and religion in Tübingen. He is the author of numerous books and articles, many of them concerned with the relation between Church and State. His books include *Menschenrechte–auch in der Kirche?* (1976) and *Kirche und Staat: Handbuch der Christlichen Ethik* (^{2}1979).

DAVID VAN OOIJEN, OP, was born in 1939 in Kwintsheul in the Netherlands. He taught in schools until 1961, when he entered the Dominican Order, becoming a priest in 1968. He studied theology at the University of Nijmegen, obtaining his doctorate in 1971. He was also elected as a member of the Dutch Lower House, standing for the socialist Partij van de Arbeid, in 1971. From 1973 until 1978, he was a member of the advisory assembly of the Council of Europe and the Western European Union. In parliament, he is mainly concerned with educational and cultural affairs and with the position of ethnic minorities. He is chairman of the Interparliamentary Council for Benelux, that is, the parliamentary organisation of the union between Belgium, the Netherlands and Luxembourg that was formed in 1958. His writings include: 'De identificatie van christelijke politiek en christendemocratische partijvorming' in *Mythe en Realiteit van Christelijke Politiek* (Baarn 1979); *Social Aspects of Architectural Conservation* (Strasbourg 1974); *Advanced Technology in Canada—the Consequences for Europe* (Paris 1974); *Advanced Technology in Israel—the Consequences for Europe* (Paris 1977).

A Synopsis of the Four Gospels

IN GREEK

arranged according to the two-gospel hypothesis and edited by

JOHN BERNARD ORCHARD O.S.B.

Dom Bernard Orchard's synopsis illustrates clearly the 'Two-Gospel' hypothesis, following the authorship sequence of Matthew-Luke-Mark-John and thus challenging the theory of Markan priority. In this, he creates a new angle of vision on the inter-relationships between the Gospels and even on the order of events in the life of Jesus.

". . it marks a real improvement in its treatment of textual critical problems in the Gospels . . . he shows judgement, independence, originality" (Prof. G D Kilpatrick, formerly of Queen's College, Oxford)

". . certain to be needed by all who take Gospel source criticism seriously" (Prof. R Barbour, King's College, Aberdeen)

ISBN: 0 567 09331 X   364pp   cased   £9·95

Conversations on Counselling

between a doctor and a priest

DIALOGUE & TRINITY

edited by

MARCUS LEFÉBURE

'Conversations on Counselling' initiates an examination of the still often unreflected presuppositions and values of counselling and offers a deeply experienced and thought out spiritual interpretation of counselling work.

"An invitation to eavesdrop on a very intelligent, very sensitive exploratory dialogue . . . about very complex human relationships and the role of the counsellor in them" (The Most Rev. Alastair Haggart, Bishop of Edinburgh, Primus of the Scottish Episcopal Church)

"Christian pastoral care and spiritual direction and the modern counselling movement have much to learn from each other: this book opens up the vital dialogue in a way which is profoundly serious and eminently practical" (Professor Forrester, Department of Christian Ethics and Practical Theology, University of Edinburgh)

". . an intriguing and original work . . . It is concerned with the personal experience and process of counselling. The dialogues draw out, analyse and then go beyond the counselling experience . . . they reflect in a most interesting way upon the relationships and processes within and between counselling, the self, and all real communication . . ." (Professor Gerard Rochford, Prof. of Social Work Studies, University of Aberdeen)

ISBN: 0 567 29112   112pp   paperback   £3·95

T & T Clark, 36 George Street, Edinburgh EH2 2LQ   031-225 4703

Karl Barth—Rudolf Bultmann
Letters 1922-1966

Translated by GEOFFREY W. BROMILEY

Containing all the available letters and postcards exchanged by Karl Barth and Rudolf Bultmann over a period of 44 years, this collection in many respects exceeds secondary volumes on the theology of Barth and Bultmann in its direct treatment of the central themes of Christian theology and practice. Most significantly, it traces their theological maturation as well as their major disagreements. The text is supplemented by biographical and literary notes as well as 40 other letters, cards, public declarations, memoranda and autobiographical sketches.

ISBN: 0 567 09334 4   224pp   cased   £6·95

Learning Jesus Christ through
the Heidelberg Catechism

by KARL BARTH

Karl Barth's informative introduction to an important, though largely unknown, Calvinistic document of the Reformation.
The two short studies included here
The first essay CHRISTIAN DOCTRINE ACCORDING TO THE HEIDELBERG CATECHISM is a question-by-question interpretation, commentary and evaluation of the catechism. INTRODUCTION TO THE HEIDELBERG CATECHISM, the second study, examines the three basic questions of the document: "Who is comforted? How is comfort given? In what does it consist?"
These two works also offer a brief, systematic presentation of Reformed theology in the 16th century and a glimpse of Barth's own theology in the 20th century.

ISBN: 0 8028 1893 5   (Distributed by T & T Clark for Eerdmans, USA)
144pp   paperback   £3·75

Great Themes from the Old Testament

by NORBERT LOHFINK (translated by Ronald Walls)

". . a scholar with an often original turn of mind and a skill in vivid presentation. His writings are based on sound scholarship . . . the reader is being invited to consider both very stimulating interpretations of the biblical text and also illuminating discussion of the relationship between these and contemporary religious problems" (Professor P R Ackroyd, King's College, London)
"Lohfink offers a very attractive blend of perceptive and imaginative Old Testament scholarship on the one hand and sensitivity for key contemporary issues on the other. I know of no comparable volume. The Old Testament scholarship represents the best of todays. The issues are right up to date . ." (Rev. Graeme Auld, Lecturer in Hebrew and Old Testament Studies, University of Edinburgh)

ISBN: 1 567 09333 6   270pp   cased   £7·95

T & T Clark, 36 George Street, Edinburgh EH2 2LQ   031-225 4703

CONCILIUM

Claude Geffré. 0 8164 2542 6 144pp.

87. **The Future of Christian Marriage.** Ed. William Bassett and Peter Huizing. 0 8164 2575 2.

88. **Polarization in the Church.** Ed. Hans Küng and Walter Kasper. 0 8164 2572 8 156pp.

89. **Spiritual Revivals.** Ed. Christian Duquoc and Casiano Floristán. 0 8164 2573 6 156pp.

90. **Power and the Word of God.** Ed. Franz Bockle and Jacques Marie Pohier. 0 8164 2574 4 156pp.

91. **The Church as Institution.** Ed. Gregory Baum and Andrew Greeley. 0 8164 2575 2 168pp.

92. **Politics and Liturgy.** Ed. Herman Schmidt and David Power. 0 8164 2576 0 156pp.

93. **Jesus Christ and Human Freedom.** Ed. Edward Schillebeeckx and Bas van Iersel. 0 8164 2577 9 168pp.

94. **The Experience of Dying.** Ed. Norbert Greinacher and Alois Müller. 0 8164 2578 7 156pp.

95. **Theology of Joy.** Ed. Johannes Baptist Metz and Jean-Pierre Jossua. 0 8164 2579 5 164pp.

96. **The Mystical and Political Dimension of the Christian Faith.** Ed. Claude Geffré and Gustavo Guttierez. 0 8164 2580 9 168pp.

97. **The Future of the Religious Life.** Ed. Peter Huizing and William Bassett. 0 8164 2094 7 96pp.

98. **Christians and Jews.** Ed. Hans Küng and Walter Kasper. 0 8164 2095 5 96pp.

99. **Experience of the Spirit.** Ed. Peter Huizing and William Bassett. 0 8164 2096 3 144pp.

100. **Sexuality in Contemporary Catholicism.** Ed. Franz Bockle and Jacques Marie Pohier. 0 8164 2097 1 126pp.

101. **Ethnicity.** Ed. Andrew Greeley and Gregory Baum. 0 8164 2145 5 120pp.

102. **Liturgy and Cultural Religious Traditions.** Ed. Herman Schmidt and David Power. 0 8164 2146 2 120pp.

103. **A Personal God?** Ed. Edward Schillebeeckx and Bas van Iersel. 0 8164 2149 8 142pp.

104. **The Poor and the Church.** Ed. Norbert Greinacher and Alois Müller. 0 8164 2147 1 128pp.

105. **Christianity and Socialism.** Ed. Johannes Baptist Metz and Jean-Pierre Jossua. 0 8164 2148 X 144pp.

106. **The Churches of Africa: Future Prospects.** Ed. Claude Geffré and Bertrand Luneau. 0 8164 2150 1 128pp.

107. **Judgement in the Church.** Ed. William Bassett and Peter Huizing. 0 8164 2166 8 128pp.

108. **Why Did God Make Me?** Ed. Hans Küng and Jürgen Moltmann. 0 8164 2167 6 112pp.

109. **Charisms in the Church.** Ed. Christian Duquoc and Casiano Floristán. 0 8164 2168 4 128pp.

110. **Moral Formation and Christianity.** Ed. Franz Bockle and Jacques Marie Pohier. 0 8164 2169 2 120pp.

111. **Communication in the Church.** Ed. Gregory Baum and Andrew Greeley. 0 8164 2170 6 126pp.

112. **Liturgy and Human Passage.** Ed. David Power and Luis Maldonado. 0 8164 2608 2 136pp.

113. **Revelation and Experience.** Ed. Edward Schillebeeckx and Bas van Iersel. 0 8164 2609 0 134pp.

114. **Evangelization in the World Today.** Ed. Norbert Greinacher and Alois Müller. 0 8164 2610 4 136pp.

115. **Doing Theology in New Places.** Ed. Jean-Pierre Jossua and Johannes Baptist Metz. 0 8164 2611 2 120pp.

116. **Buddhism and Christianity.** Ed. Claude Geffré and Mariasusai Dhavamony. 0 8164 2612 0 136pp.

117. **The Finances of the Church.** Ed. William Bassett and Peter Huizing. 0 8164 2197 8 160pp.

118. **An Ecumenical Confession of Faith?** Ed. Hans Küng and Jürgen Moltmann. 0 8164 2198 6 136pp.

119. **Discernment of the Spirit and of Spirits.** Ed. Casiano Floristán and Christian Duquoc. 0 8164 2199 4 136pp.

120. **The Death Penalty and Torture.** Ed. Franz Bockle and Jacques Marie Pohier. 0 8164 2200 1 136pp.

121. **The Family in Crisis or in Transition.** Ed. Andrew Greely. 0 567 30001 3 128pp.

122. **Structures of Initiation in Crisis.** Ed. Luis Maldonado and David Power. 0 567 30002 1 128pp.

123. **Heaven.** Ed. Bas van Iersel and Edward Schillebeeckx. 0 567 30003 X 120pp.

124. **The Church and the Rights of Man.** Ed. Alois Müller and Norbert Greinacher. 0 567 30004 8 140pp.

125. **Christianity and the Bourgeoisie.** Ed. Johannes Baptist Metz. 0 567 30005 6 144pp.

126. **China as a Challenge to the Church.** Ed. Claude Geffré and Joseph Spae. 0 567 30006 4 136pp.

127. **The Roman Curia and the Communion of Churches.** Ed. Peter Huizing and Knut Walf. 0 567 30007 2 144pp.

128. **Conflicts about the Holy Spirit.** Ed. Hans Küng and Jürgen Moltmann. 0 567 30008 0 144pp.

129. **Models of Holiness.** Ed. Christian Duquoc and Casiano Floristán. 0 567 30009 9 128pp.

130. **The Dignity of the Despised of the Earth.** Ed. Jacques Marie Pohier and Dietmar Mieth. 0 567 30010 2 144pp.

131. **Work and Religion.** Ed. Gregory Baum. 0 567 30011 0 148pp.

132. **Symbol and Art in Worship.** Ed. Luis Maldonado and David Power. 0 567 30012 9 136pp.

133. **Right of the Community to a Priest.** Ed. Edward Schillebeeckx and Johannes Baptist Metz. 0 567 30013 7 148pp.

134. **Women in a Men's Church.** Ed. Virgil Elizondo and Norbert Greinacher. 0 567 30014 5 144pp.

135. **True and False Universality of Christianity.** Ed. Claude Geffré and Jean-Pierre Jossua. 0 567 30015 3 138pp.

136. **What is Religion? An Inquiry for Christian Theology.** Ed. Mircea Eliade and David Tracy. 0 567 30016 1 98pp.

137. **Electing our Own Bishops.** Ed. Peter Huizing and Knut Walf. 0 567 30017 X 112pp.

138. **Conflicting Ways of Interpreting the Bible.** Ed. Hans Küng and Jürgen Moltmann. 0 567 30018 8 112pp.

139. **Christian Obedience.** Ed. Casiano Floristán and Christian Duquoc. 0 567 30019 6 96pp.

140. **Christian Ethics and Economics: the North-South Conflict.** Ed. Dietmar Mieth and Jacques Marie Pohier. 0 567 30020 X 128pp.

1981

141. **Neo-Conservatism: Social and Religious Phenomenon.** Ed. Gregory Baum and John Coleman. 0 567 30021 8.

142. **The Times of Celebration.** Ed. David Power and Mary Collins. 0 567 30022 6.

143. **God as Father.** Ed. Edward Schillebeeckx and Johannes Baptist Metz. 0 567 30023 4.

144. **Tensions Between the Churches of the First World and the Third World.** Ed. Virgil Elizondo and Norbert Greinacher. 0 567 30024 2.

145. **Nietzsche and Christianity.** Ed. Claude Geffré and Jean-Pierre Jossua. 0 567 30025 0.

146. **Where Does the Church Stand?** Ed. Giuseppe Alberigo. 0 567 30026 9.

147. **The Revised Code of Canon Law: a Missed Opportunity?** Ed. Peter Huizing and Knut Walf. 0 567 30027 7.

148. **Who Has the Say in the Church?** Ed. Hans Küng and Jürgen Moltmann. 0 567 30028 5.

149. **Francis of Assisi Today.** Ed. Casiano Floristán and Christian Duquoc. 0 567 30029 3.

150. **Christian Ethics: Uniformity, Universality, Pluralism.** Ed. Jacques Pohier and Dietmar Mieth. 0 567 30030 7.

All back issues are still in print and available for sale. Orders should be sent to the publishers,

T. & T. CLARK LIMITED
36 George Street, Edinburgh EH2 2LQ, Scotland